CREATED FOR INTIMACY

CREATED FOR INTIMACY

John and Agnes Sturt

eagle
Guildford, Surrey

British Library Cataloguing in Publication Data. A catalogue
record for this book is available from the British Library.

Published by Eagle, an imprint of Inter Publishing Service
(IPS) Ltd, St Nicholas House, 14 The Mount, Guildford, Surrey
GU2 5HN.

Typeset by Palimpsest Book Production Limited,
Polmont, Stirlingshire

Printed by Caledonian International Book Manufacturing

ISBN No: 0 86347 188 9

TABLE OF CONTENTS

FOREWORD

Intimacy, like a long, cool drink on an oven-hot day, is something most people crave for much of their lives. Yet the merging of our mind and emotions with another and the oneness of body and spirit that we yearn for can seem as elusive as water in the desert. That's why many readers may turn for help to this book.

In it the authors have drawn on their long and extensive experience of working with couples, individuals and with themselves to answer some of the questions that burn in our hearts when the longing for intimacy is acute. Questions like: 'Why do I find it so hard to experience oneness with others?', '*How* do I enjoy intimacy with another?', 'Why does loneliness sometimes yawn inside me like a bottomless chasm?'

The elixir of intimacy is so deeply renewing that seeking answers to such questions is time well spent. John and Agnes Sturt help us to use such time creatively by suggesting ways of finding tailor-made answers that could contain healing and wholeness. Those who work at the exercises will doubtless gain most from the book.

Their readers will be grateful to them for the painstaking and thorough way with which they have dealt with a difficult and sensitive subject. They are well qualified to do so because of the way they themselves have worked at the tasks they set their readers. We make that claim because we know them to be a couple with a capacity for creating intimacy with a whole variety of people.

John and Agnes drove into our lives in 1990 in New Zealand where they live. We had been relaxing in someone's holiday home by the sea. John and Agnes kindly collected us from our hideaway and drove us back to

Auckland. Within minutes, it seemed, we gelled as a four.
In fact, it seemed as though we had been friends for years.
A few weeks later they hosted a Marriage Weekend where
we were the Guest Speakers. There we watched them relate
to several hurting people and were impressed by their care
for others as well as by their insights.

On a subsequent visit to New Zealand, we became
guests in the Sturts' home. There we met, not only their
grown-up children but some of their grandchildren as
well. The mutuality they shared with offspring of all
ages was delightful. Even more delightful was the obvious oneness they enjoy with each other. In other words,
we have witnessed them practising what they preach in
this book. Although they are both busy, creative, gifted,
fulfilled people in their own right, they ear-mark time for
a variety of relationships: supremely, with God, with each
other and with their immediate family – but with friends
and strangers too. In fact, they have a gift of hospitality
and their beautiful home is a haven for many. Somehow
they have managed to avoid the trap they highlight in
this book:

*'In our materialistic society there is a temptation to love things
and use people. Friendship and intimacy only become priorities
when we love people and use things.'*

John and Agnes love people – many people. They confess
in this book, however, that such intimacies have not necessarily come easily. Some have been hard-earned. That's
comforting for those of us who still struggle to learn
the difficult arts of loving, communicating and giving
ourselves to others.

In a book of this size, it is impossible to provide an
in-depth study of subjects as complex as friendship, loneliness and intimacy with God to mention but three of
the topics covered. Some readers will therefore find that
their appetites are whetted enough to turn to the helpful
bibliography to discover where and how they can further
plumb the depths of such mysteries. At the same time, they
may well find themselves carrying from this book kernels

of truth on which they can meditate for themselves – gems like this one:

'*The strength of true friendship is love and caring, a desire for the other's good rather than personal advantage. When this attitude is mutual, friendship blossoms.*'

Throughout the book, John and Agnes point the way to the architect of intimacy: God. Words of a chorus have been throbbing through Joyce's mind while she read this manuscript:

'Tell my people I love them
Tell my people I care
When they feel far away from me
Tell my people I'm there.'

Sometimes such intimacy with God comes to us direct through prayer or through watching a stunning sunset or through meditating on words from the Bible. Sometimes it comes through precious people. Our prayer for those who read and use this book – singles and marrieds alike – is that it *will* come – for herein lies the source of the intimacy that has healing in its wings.

Joyce and David Huggett
Cyprus 1996

ACKNOWLEDGEMENTS

This book has been years in the making, as much of it reflects our own journey. On this journey, many people have influenced our lives through their model of good relationships. Books, too, have influenced our thinking and personal growth, and we owe much to the wisdom of writers in the field of human relationships. We acknowledge this throughout these pages.

Specifically, we wish to thank the following for their help in the preparation of this book. Dr Hans Everts of Auckland University Department of Education helped us in the design of the intimacy survey, and Chris Twyman, used his magic computer skills to analyse the results. We are grateful to the three hundred participants in our survey for the gifts of their time and themselves.

A number of people have reviewed portions of the book or contributed in other ways. In particular we thank Joyce and David Huggett, Sue Wavre, Peter Lineham, Sheila Pritchard, Richard Charmley, Ivan Howie, Carolyn Manning, Margaret Corrin, Cilla Potter, John Cooney, Steve and Elaine McFadzean, Anthea Harper, Ranee Gedye, Jocelyn Grantham and Graeme Packer, and Pat Bish for the cover design.

To

Barbara and Colin, Alison and Roger, Carol and Grant
with whom we have shared friendship and intimacy in
different ways and on different days of our journey.

INTRODUCTION

INTIMACY is the peak experience of human relationships. To really know another person and to be known brings meaning and fulfilment to life. The ability to be intimate is related to our level of maturity, as we deal with our intra-personal and inter-personal tensions and conflicts. Intimacy is also the goal of our relationship with God.[1] But intimacy with people or with God is not automatic. It has to be desired and worked for. There are principles upon which healthy intimacy is based.

Many people long for intimacy but do not know how to find it. Others go about it in self-defeating ways. Some people are not even aware that intimacy is possible, while others have been so badly hurt in their search for intimacy that they have settled for life without it. If you are interested in how to be close to another person, whether you are single or married, this book may help you.

TWO MAIN SECTIONS

In **PART I** we examine the foundations of intimacy and seek to answer a number of questions. Why is intimacy so important to us as human beings? Are there cultural and gender differences in attitudes to intimacy? What factors in our society make intimacy difficult? What factors within us as individuals prevent us from experiencing the intimacy we desire?

The basic principles of intimacy are explored and some blocks and keys to intimacy defined. The ability to make an intimate relationship with another starts with a sense of self-worth. If I don't know myself, and especially if I don't like myself, I will certainly not want to share myself with others. Chapter five deals with this issue, and the whole area of self-esteem has been developed in depth in our companion book, *Created for Love*.[2]

PART II explores how intimacy can be experienced in singleness, in marriage, and in our relationship with God. The basic principles of intimacy with people and with God are the same. Experiencing human intimacy prepares us for intimacy with God, and intimacy with him transforms human relationships.

A NEW ZEALAND SURVEY

In order to obtain a broader perspective, we conducted a written survey of 300 people. This was an attempt to obtain objective data on the attitudes and experience of a range of people in the areas of loneliness, friendship and intimacy. The results have been analysed thoroughly and some of these are included in various chapters. Brief comments on the survey are in Appendix 2, and anyone interested in further details could write to us.

A PRACTICAL WORK BOOK

Created for Intimacy is not a theoretical book but is a practical manual of *how to* develop friendship and intimacy. At the end of each chapter are questions and specific exercises for those who wish to work on issues raised. These are designed to help you explore your own experience of intimacy and to develop greater intimacy in your relationships. This *work book* can be used on your own or with a 'travelling companion', trusted friend, counsellor, mentor or in a small growth group. There is great value in being part of a *growth group*, and working through this book in such a situation is a good way to make use of it.

We also recommend that you keep a *journal*, or notebook, as you read this book. Record the answers to questions and exercises, as well as the insights and feelings you have as you work through the material. This will become a valuable record of your personal journey in the area of relationships and intimacy. Using a journal is an effective way to obtain a clearer perspective on life. We find it helps us to be in touch with our own reality, and also to encounter other people and God. A journal provides a mirror on life, reflecting your journey to wholeness. 'In its pages we may find a moving image which represents who I have been, who I am now, and who I am becoming.'[3]

CREATED FOR INTIMACY

We are created for intimacy and not designed to live in isolation. The experience of intimacy is elusive but can be a reality for us all. It is our sincere desire and prayer that this book will encourage you in your search for a deeper experience of intimacy in your relationships with people and with God.

John and Agnes Sturt
15a Warborough Avenue,
Auckland,
New Zealand,
1996

PART ONE

FOUNDATIONS OF INTIMACY

The first seven chapters look at our human need for close relationships and various factors which either help or hinder the achievement of intimacy.

Chapter 1
Loneliness is explored in terms of its origin, effects on the human personality and its ultimate purpose. There are two basic forms of loneliness: relational and existential. Loneliness must also be distinguished from aloneness and solitude.

Chapter 2
Friendship is defined and its principles are explored, particularly the attitudes and values that are needed for a good relationship. Important skills that are required to build a good friendship are outlined.

Chapter 3
This chapter explores the meaning and range of intimacy between people. This is illustrated by results from our survey. The main determinant of our ability to enjoy intimacy is our own personal history and modelling. We also look at gender differences.

Chapter 4
Historical and cultural factors in our background have a big effect on our ability to experience intimacy. Negative

attitudes of men towards women will block intimacy between the genders. These issues are explored, with particular reference to their effect on Western society.

Chapter 5
Intimacy with another person presupposes experiencing intimacy within. This means that I must come to know and value myself before I will be able to reveal myself to another. This chapter explores a number of ways of knowing and developing yourself.

Chapter 6
Before we can experience intimacy in relationships we need to deal with potential 'road blocks' within us. The five main ones are: poor self-awareness and psychological defences; low self-esteem; negative attitudes and distorted thinking about intimacy; differences between people; inadequate relationship skills.

Chapter 7
Three main keys to intimacy are: a commitment to making intimacy a priority; becoming 'other-centred' and learning how to share yourself. Sharing yourself with another person involves removing 'masks' appropriately and learning how to reveal and receive feelings. Intimacy develops best between two whole people.

ONE

LONELINESS

I lie awake, lonely as a solitary sparrow on the roof.
David, c. 1000 BC[1]

The voice on the other end of the phone was flat and expressionless. I greeted her cheerfully, but this only seemed to increase her gloom. It was Christmas Eve and Catherine was alone in a dingy flat. She had recently emigrated from England, but soon after arriving in New Zealand with high hopes of making a new life here, her husband deserted her for another woman.

Catherine told me she had no money, no job, no friends or family in this country. The Christmas season only served to heighten her sense of loneliness and isolation, and suicide seemed a very real option to her. We talked for two hours. Later that evening I finished my telephone shift at the community counselling agency and returned home to my wife and family. That telephone conversation made me profoundly aware of the destructiveness of loneliness, and also of our responsibility as human beings to be sensitive to loneliness in the lives of people around us.

We all know what it is like to be lonely, even if we have not experienced such devastation as Catherine. Loneliness is hard to describe. Dictionaries define it in such terms as: without company or companionship; destitute of friendly relationships. But these descriptions are incomplete. Loneliness occurs mostly when we miss the company of other people, but we can also feel lonely when we are *with* people. At other times we may be alone without feeling lonely. For most of us, loneliness is an intense short-lived experience, but for some it is an aspect of life from which they are seldom free.

WHAT IS LONELINESS?

Over the past thirty years, many studies have been made on the phenomenon of loneliness and a significant amount of literature is available on the subject. Probably the best definition of loneliness is that put forward by Drs Peplau and Perlman, researchers at the University of California in Los Angeles. They define loneliness as: 'The emotional response a person has to a perceived discrepancy between expected and achieved levels of social contact.'[2]

What these authors are saying is that loneliness begins when you receive from other people in your social network less than what you expect from them. This explains why people who seldom experience friendship or intimacy at work may not feel lonely there. But the same people may feel very lonely if they receive little intimacy from a marriage partner, from whom they expect much more.

Self-reported loneliness is highest among adolescents and declines significantly with increasing age.[3] Part of the reason for this is that young people typically have much greater, and possibly more unrealistic, expectations of their social relationships than older people have.

But the main determinant of loneliness, that emerged in a number of studies, is not the presence or absence of people but a lack of intimate relationships in a person's life. Thus, it is important to have some understanding of loneliness before discussing intimacy. If I am afraid to face the pain of my loneliness I cannot achieve intimacy.

Loneliness is accompanied by a range of feelings that vary with the circumstances. Some feelings that people have used to describe their loneliness are: miserable, sad, rejected, abandoned, insecure, uncertain, hurt, numb, empty, worthless, depressed, angry, fearful, panicky, hopeless. One of the most famous loners in literature is Robinson Crusoe. He described his experience as: 'absolutely miserable, abandoned, so entirely depressed it could hardly be rational to be thankful for such a life.'[4] Loneliness is frequently linked with depression, though depressed people are not always lonely. Loneliness differs from aloneness, in that the former is associated with *unpleasant* feelings, but the latter usually is not.

Loneliness is a universal human experience. It is something which people may fear as a great evil and try to avoid at all costs. Many studies have shown that loneliness is associated with problems such as alcoholism, substance abuse, adolescent delinquent behaviour, depression and suicide. The ultimate form of mental torture in oppressive regimes is forced solitary confinement. But this term aptly describes the lifestyle of so many people in our society today: self-imposed solitary confinement. They may not have chosen it consciously, but neither do they know how to escape from it.

Loneliness is a growing phenomenon in our civilization and a major social problem of modern life. The more people congregate in large urban sprawls, the more loneliness is evident in society. Isaiah anticipated this happening in about 750 BC: 'Woe to you who add house to house and join field to field till no space is left and you live alone in the land.'[5] How sad that loneliness is still one of the hallmarks of Western Christian society, which was founded on the love of God and love for one's neighbour.

At the turn of the twentieth century approximately eighty per cent of the world's population lived in villages or rural areas, where most people had a sense of belonging and knew their neighbours for miles around. By the beginning of the twenty-first century over half of all human beings will be living in towns and megacities, where they may not even know the names of people in the unit next door.

We live in Auckland, a city of over one million people. Surveys have shown that at least twenty-five per cent of residences in Auckland have only one person living in them. Similar statistics are reported from most Western countries. While some people live alone because of circumstances outside their control, most people who live on their own choose to do so.

We sometimes conduct spot checks on groups of 100 cars that we pass consecutively as we drive along. Eighty-five to ninety per cent have only one person in them. This does not mean that everyone living alone or travelling on their own is lonely, but it does say something about the modern Western lifestyle and its link with loneliness. This is explored further in chapter four.

Children can experience quite severe degrees of loneliness, even if brought up in secure and happy families. I (Agnes) grew up on a farm in a family of five children, with uncles, aunts and cousins nearby. We also knew other families well within a radius of several miles. I attended a small country school with about thirty pupils and one teacher. Older children helped the younger ones, like a big family.

For secondary education I boarded at a large city high school, where I experienced extreme loneliness. I felt bewildered, confused and disorientated in a school of so many pupils, and was teased for being so shy. I'll never forget the longings for my family and familiar home environment. Other girls didn't seem to feel this way, or if they did, they did not show it. It took me a long time to develop a sense of belonging at that school. I felt so alone in a crowd. At night I shared a dormitory with a dozen others, but longed for the security of a place that was my own. An intense experience of loneliness in childhood may affect us in later life.

Loneliness and the need for friendship have been the subject of books, poetry, songs and plays over the centuries. The ancient Greek philosophers often spoke on this theme. Each generation must address these issues in the light of changes in its society, but the deep longing for closeness and intimacy has never changed.

MEDICAL AND SOCIAL EFFECTS OF LONELINESS

Loneliness not only affects the quality of our lives but also our health and life expectancy. Dr James Lynch has conducted extensive research into the effects of human loneliness on the illnesses and death rates of people of all races in the United States.[6] He writes:

> The *broken heart* is not just a poetic image for loneliness and despair but is an overwhelming medical reality. All the available data points to the lack of human companionship, chronic loneliness, social isolation, and the sudden loss of a loved one as being among the leading causes of premature death in the United States. While we found that the effects of human loneliness were related to virtually every major disease – whether cancer, pneumonia, or mental illness – they were particularly apparent in heart disease, the leading cause of death in the United States. Evidently, millions of people were dying, quite literally, of broken or lonely hearts.[7]

It has been repeatedly demonstrated by researchers in various parts of the world that the death rate, from almost all causes, is higher in single, widowed or divorced people than in married individuals.

A community study in Dunedin, New Zealand, found that teenagers were the age group most likely to experience loneliness.[8] It is significant that teenagers and young adults (fifteen- to twenty-four-year-olds) also have the highest suicide rate in this country.[9]

The study revealed that the loneliest periods for most people occurred at times of major life changes, such as a new job, a relationship break-up, or moving away from home. But despite the link between life events and loneliness, nearly half the subjects in the study felt responsible for their most lonely periods, and saw 'the sort of person I

am' as part of the problem. This was particularly true for
the ones who felt most lonely.

The most interesting point which emerged from the
study was that *the quality of contacts with close friends*
was more important than the quantity of contact. The
chief predictors of loneliness identified were: how close
the person was to the closest person in his/her life, how
many close friends they had, and how satisfied they were
with their relationships. In other words, the experience of
real intimacy in a person's life is the key to prevention of
loneliness. The less intimacy, the more loneliness a person
is likely to experience.

This conclusion was confirmed in our own survey on
intimacy. Of the group of seventeen respondents who
identified themselves as experiencing daily loneliness, 100
per cent of them claimed that emotional closeness to others
was vital or very important. Only thirty-five per cent of
the same group regarded social interaction important.
The answer to loneliness is not merely social contact but
intimate relationships.

IN THE BEGINNING

When God created this world, he saw all he had made and
concluded that it was very good.[10] But soon afterwards God
identified one thing that was *not good* in that perfect world:
loneliness.

> It is not good for the man to be alone.
> I will make a helper suitable for him. (Genesis 2:18)

The word 'man' here is the Hebrew word *adam*, which
means human being, or mankind, both male and female.
This is in distinction to the next use of the word 'man' in v
23, which is the Hebrew word *iysh*, meaning male person. So
God is not so much saying in v 18 that Adam needed a wife
and female counterpart (which of course was true) but that

human beings were made for companionship. According to our Maker, we are not designed to go through life alone.

Human beings are created in the image of God who said, 'Let us make man in our image, in our likeness.'[11] God lives in community: Father, Son and Holy Spirit, and we have been created with this same capacity for relationship. In fact, we are incomplete as human beings if we try to face life totally on our own. This does not mean that marriage is the answer to loneliness. As counsellors, we meet just as many lonely married people as lonely singles. Jesus lived life to the full as a single person. So did Paul. But the text is saying that God did not create us to live in isolation, without significant relationships or without intimacy. Joyce Huggett writes: Human beings must have intimacy. Whether we recognise it or not, within each of us there is a powerful longing to create a really deep relationship with at least one other person.[12]

TWO KINDS OF LONELINESS

Relational Loneliness

We have been designed by God for relationship. A person's life is not complete without a significant relationship with another human being. The Bible is primarily about relationships not theology. It defines the principles of how to relate to God and to others. Scripture records hundreds of case histories, showing how people related to God and to their fellows. They are certainly not all success stories, because the Bible is totally honest in its account of people's lives. In fact, many of the relationships described were disasters! Paul tells us that the reason they are recorded is to provide warnings for us.[13] We are foolish if we do not learn from the past.

Theology arises out of this need for relationship, and the message of the Bible is all about how we can relate to God and improve our relationships with people. When we personally discovered this principle of understanding Scripture it took on fresh meaning and relevance. We have learned much about good communication and healthy relationships from a study of this 'text book'. Most insights reported in the past three or four decades in books on sociology, counselling and human potential are principles already defined in Scripture, at least in essence. So we make no apology for drawing freely on this source of wisdom.

There are two forms of relational loneliness:

A) Living-Alone-Loneliness (LAL)
This refers to people who are isolated in society, who usually live on their own. Not all people who live alone are lonely. Some are gregarious and have lots of friends. But many people in our cities who live alone are desperately lonely. It was primarily among people suffering from LAL that medical researchers have found such high rates of physical illness.

B) Living-Together-Loneliness (LTL)
It is generally assumed that married people will not be lonely. Many people see freedom from loneliness as a reason for getting married. But marriage of itself does not solve loneliness, only intimacy does. At a certain basic level, living together obviously provides companionship and someone to talk to. But many people who share the same house and the same bed are unable to share their inner selves. This can lead to devastating loneliness. Our survey results showed that married women were more often lonely than single women, and married men more often than single men.

Psychotherapist Dr Dan Kiley has made a study of this problem which he describes in his book: *Living Together, Feeling Alone*.[14] He found that many of his clients suffered from living-together-loneliness. LTL is mostly experienced by women, though perhaps men are less able to identify it or acknowledge it. He believes it has only emerged as a major problem within the past twenty years or so. The probable reason for this is that *expectations* placed on marriage have changed over the past few years.

Traditional expectations were that marriage would provide security and children, but not necessarily intimacy and
emotional closeness. Husband and wife roles were more
rigidly defined, with the man as bread-winner and the
woman home-maker. Couples may have been disappointed
if they did not feel close as well, but without a strong
expectation of closeness in marriage they did not experience
so much loneliness. This fits in with the Peplau and Perlman
definition of loneliness quoted earlier. We will return to the
implications of living-together-loneliness when discussing
intimacy in marriage in chapter nine.

Loneliness often reflects a deficiency in social and communication skills. This is one of the factors responsible
for high rates of loneliness reported among adolescents,
who are still acquiring these skills. Yet the experience of
loneliness has its positive side in that it can be a driving
force to do something about it. It has been demonstrated
in experimental studies with undergraduate students that
situationally lonely subjects became more successful as
communicators than non-lonely subjects. This is attribu-
table to an increase in the motivation to relate that lonely
situations produce.[15]

The answer to relational loneliness lies not only in
the discovery of the principles of good communication
and friendship. It also requires the conviction that it is
worthwhile leaving the 'comfort zone' of self-protection
and having the courage to reach out to others. I have to
move out of the safety of my 'world-of-one', and change
from being self-centred to becoming *other-centred*. In the
process, I may well be hurt by other people who are also
struggling with their loneliness and relationships. We all
make mistakes as we learn, but the quest is worth the effort
required.

Existential Loneliness

This refers to a loneliness that is universal. It is a deep
awareness that I am ultimately alone in this world, even

though I may experience intimacy with another person on a regular basis. It is inherent in the very nature of human existence. We are all unique individuals. I am *me* and you are *you* and we are both alone in the universe. Nobody can really know my pain or joy. St Paul said, 'No one can really know what anyone else is thinking, or what he is really like, except that person himself.'[16] I came into the world alone and ultimately must leave it on my own. An old African proverb puts it: 'The earth is a beehive. We all enter by the same door but live in different cells.'

Existential loneliness is built into us in order to draw us to God and it alerts us to our need of him. There is a God-shaped space within the heart of every person. St Augustine expressed this in his famous prayer, 'Thou hast made us for Thyself and our hearts are restless until they find their rest in Thee.'[17] We can enjoy relationships and companionship with other human beings, but only in God do we find the answer to our deep existential loneliness.

People respond to existential loneliness in many ways. Some move into a life of frantic activism, endless superficial socialising, seeking fun and diversion. Others become preoccupied with material things in a relentless search for money and power. For many it takes the form of workaholism, trying to justify their existence by doing something useful, looking for meaning through work.

Busyness is probably the most usual way we distract ourselves from loneliness. It leaves no time to think about the deeper issues of life. Other popular escapes are through alcohol, substance abuse, food and sexual promiscuity. Pornography and prostitution appeal to some as an answer to loneliness because they appear to offer instant intimacy, without the risks of relationship.

Some try to meet this deep need by developing a neurotic dependence on another individual, hoping that this person will solve their problem. Others move to the other extreme, becoming rescuers of needy people. They spend their lives trying to satisfy their own needs, but trying to solve my needs through meeting yours is not helping either of us.

All these attempts to deal with inner loneliness are 'broken cisterns'[18] and serve only to keep us from the real answer. They all represent a spiritual quest, a search for solutions to our existential loneliness.

Researchers have shown consistently that religious belief not only leads to a sense of purpose, meaning and satisfaction with life but also results in less loneliness. On the other hand, non-religious people were found to be significantly more likely to experience lack of companionship, feel completely alone and unable to reach out and communicate, feeling emotionally distant from people.[19] This is not surprising. Millions of people have found that in Christ, God meets their existential human loneliness. Jesus said: 'Here I am! I stand at the door and knock. If anyone hears my voice and opens the door, I will go in and eat with him and he with me.'[20]

The significance of eating together would not have been missed by first-century readers of this word picture. In the East, those who eat together are friends and companions. Jesus uses this metaphor to express the quality of relationship that he offers. He desires to be our companion. The English word 'companion' comes from two Latin words: *com* meaning with, and *panis* meaning bread; that is, people who eat together. Jesus longs for this companionship even more than we do. He said, 'I will eat with him' (eating our bread and sharing our life), 'and he with me' (eating his bread and sharing his life). This companionship will meet our existential loneliness. And he has promised, 'Never will I leave you; never will I forsake you.'[21]

Jesus and Loneliness

Jesus experienced *relational* loneliness as a man on earth. He knew the pain and loneliness of being misunderstood by his own family.[22] Many enthusiastic disciples, who once hung on his every word, deserted him.[23] His best friends ran away in his hour of need.[24] He even experienced the horror of *existential* loneliness (separation from his Father)

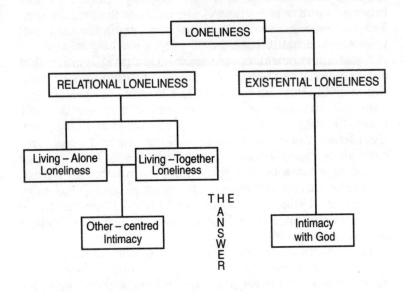

Figure 1. Types of loneliness

as he bore the sin of the world on the cross: 'My God, my God, why have you forsaken me.'[25]

In times of severe loneliness we can rejoice that Jesus empathises with our suffering. 'He is able to sympathise with our weaknesses' having been 'tempted in every way, just as we are.'[26] As we deal with loneliness, we can draw on his understanding and strength to see us through.

ALONENESS AND SOLITUDE

Self-reporting surveys have shown that adolescents and adults spend about a quarter of their waking hours alone. Over a lifetime this adds up to many years of alone time. Aloneness is not synonymous with loneliness. Sometimes they go together in the way that Catherine was both lonely and alone in her flat on Christmas Eve. But aloneness can be a deliberate choice. While we need to *be with* people, we also need *space from* people at times. It is in these times of aloneness that we can commune with ourselves and with God, assess our values and goals, be in touch with what is really happening within us, and experience rest and self-renewal. Aloneness does not produce inertia, it energises us; it can be a friend and ally. Optimum emotional health needs both intimacy and autonomy.

In our survey, ninety-two per cent of respondents said that they enjoyed being alone. *Some of the reasons given were that aloneness provides*:

- Balance and perspective to life.
- Time out from people.
- Time to relax and 're-charge batteries'.
- Time to meditate and pray.
- Opportunity for hobbies, music, reading.
- A chance to be 'just me'.

Alone times can be very beneficial. Most people find that their concentration improves when they are on their own and they can deal with complicated tasks more effectively. A person's general mood is usually somewhat depressed when alone, but some dimensions of mood rise to levels higher than normal after rejoining the company of others. It has been found that adolescents often use solitude creatively, and young people who spend more time alone show greater purpose and personal direction in their lives. When we are alone, we can process significant events, deal with grief or disappointments and grow emotionally.

We define solitude as *chosen aloneness*, as opposed to times during the day when we happen to be alone. Solitude provides opportunity to commune with ourselves and with God; a chance to grow in relationship with ourselves and with him. We need to ensure that there are islands of solitude in the sea of our busyness. Without a quiet centre, a still point, our lives will be like 'chasing after the wind'.[27] It is possible to draw into one's centre during a busy day and find stillness, like the 'eye' of a storm which is a calm centre surrounded by chaos. Loneliness hurts, solitude heals.

Henri Nouwen wrote: 'When you are able to create a lonely place in the middle of your actions and concerns, your successes and failures slowly can lose some of their power over you.'[28] Aloneness is nothing to be afraid of, but it can be scary at times, as we look into ourselves and discover who we really are. We may not always like what we see!

Solitude does not draw us away from people. Rather, it prepares us for genuine, compassionate encounter with others. A number of authors and researchers have commented on this: 'It is this capacity for inner solitude, the ability to enjoy constructive privacy, that forms the foundation upon which genuine intimacy is based.'[29] Henri Nouwen describes solitude as 'that holy place where ministry and spirituality embrace each other'.[30]

To enjoy solitude you must be comfortable with yourself, which in turn prepares you to be comfortable with others. Conversely, experiencing deep intimacy with someone else increases our ability to enjoy solitude without experiencing loneliness. 'Your capacity for solitude, for feeling comfortable with yourself, exists on a continuum with your capacity for intimacy – being in good contact with others.'[31]

It is also in solitude that we have the best opportunity to encounter God. When we meet God in solitude, it can be an awesome, life-changing experience. Thomas Merton wrote: 'It is in silence, and not in commotion, in solitude and not in crowds, that God best likes to reveal himself.'[32] Elijah saw God in action among the crowds on Mt Carmel, but heard him speak to him in a gentle whisper only when he was alone on Mt Horeb.[33] He discovered his true strength in quietness and trust.[34]

Jesus often withdrew to a solitary place to be away from people and spend time alone with his Father.[35] If Jesus needed solitude and communion with his Father in his hectic schedule, how much more do we need to find time for this in our busy lives today. Carl Jung called solitude the 'fount of healing'.[36] But it is probably the experience of most of us that the busier our programme the less time we set aside for quiet renewal to be centred and focussed.

Sometimes we may experience a prolonged period of isolation which has not been of our choosing. It may be a physical or emotional event, and has been called a 'desert experience'. It can be a very important and significant time.

Desert Experiences

Time in the desert was the literal experience for many of the great characters of the Bible, notably Abraham, Moses, Elijah, David, John the Baptist and Paul. It has been an important part of the spiritual journey of many people down through the centuries. Jesus experienced forty days of solitude and fasting in the desert before embarking on his ministry. The story of the exodus of the Israelites from Egypt describes how God used this method to prepare a whole nation for the strenuous and disciplined task of capturing the promised land. But we are told that he was also developing their inner maturity.[37]

Many of us have been through a desert experience at some time in our lives. It could have been because of illness or accident, the loss of a loved one through death, the breakdown of a marriage, a business failure, being misunderstood by family or friends. It may have been devastating for us, or it could have been a time when we developed maturity and character. We have personally observed that illnesses such as depression, emotional burnout or even a terminal condition have been turning points for many people, and the start of their journey towards wholeness.[38]

A desert experience may not be associated with an external crisis. It can be a crisis in your own inner spiritual journey which you are walking alone. It may be part of a deepening awareness and discovery of who you are, which for many people occurs in mid-life. Outwardly you may not be lonely, but you may feel very much alone on your inner journey, unable to share it with anyone. It sometimes happens to one partner in a marriage relationship, or to both of them at different times. This can lead to misunderstanding and pain, requiring tolerance and acceptance from both.

Summary

Loneliness can be a destructive experience, damaging our health and well being. But relational loneliness can motivate us to better communication and to become other-centred. Existential loneliness can draw us to God. We would be the poorer without loneliness. In a sense it is a gift from God, not to cause pain but to alert us to our need for intimacy. Loneliness has been called 'a friend in disguise.'[39] But whether loneliness becomes creative or destructive in our lives depends on the choices we make in response to it.[40]

REFLECTIONS AND EXERCISES

1. LONELINESS How often are you aware of loneliness? Indicate where you would place yourself on this continuum:

< · LONELINESS ·>

1	2	3	4	5	6	7	8	9	10
DAILY				OCCASIONALLY					SELDOM

2. At times when you feel lonely, which of these are you most likely to do? (You may identify with more than one answer.)

   a) Withdraw into yourself _____
   b) Become preoccupied in a solitary activity, e.g. read a book _____
   c) Seek out someone to spend time with _____
   d) Busy yourself with work or a diversion _____
   e) Eat something _____
   f) Other _____
   _____

   • If you belong to a sharing group, discuss your answers. Identify the coping mechanisms you have in common with others and those which are unique to you.

3. SOLITUDE Do you set aside times regularly for aloneness and solitude, in order to commune with yourself and/or with God?

   • If so, do you think you spend enough time on your own? How could these times be improved?
   • If the idea of having regular times of solitude is new to you, are you willing to try it? What things, or people, in your life would make this difficult and

might sabotage your attempts? What steps would you need to take to ensure that you will have times of aloneness on a regular basis?

4. Choose a quiet place in your home, or perhaps in the garden, where you will not be disturbed. Relax. Take some slow deep breaths. Repeat the words of Psalm 46:10 a few times: 'Be still and know that I am God.' Focus on God and enjoy him. Listen to what he might want to say to you.

5. DESERT EXPERIENCES   Make a study of instances in the Bible where notable characters experienced times of prolonged solitude or a period in the desert. What purpose do you think it served in their lives? What can you learn from this?

6. Have you had a time in your life where you felt as if you were in a 'desert place'? What caused this?

   • What emotions did you feel and how did it affect you?
   • What did you learn from it?
   • Would you have reacted differently with hindsight?
   • What can you thank God for as you look back on that experience?

TWO

FRIENDSHIP

A faithful friend is the medicine of life.
                                    Ben Sira, 180 BC[1]
Without friends no one would choose to live, even if he had
                    all other goods.
                                    Aristotle, 384–322 BC[2]

I t is friendship, not love, which makes the world go round.
From early childhood we all desire the company and
friendship of others. Human beings have an innate desire
for relationships. Anthropologists assert that friendship is
a universal characteristic of all human societies, and all
cultures emphasise the essential loyalty and love between
friends.[3] Healthy human development requires the stimulation of interaction with others, resulting in friendship and
in some cases deep intimacy.

Thankyou for friends
        and companions on the Way,
For the richness of the meeting of two minds,
For the growth and life that comes
        from being challenged
        to imagine new horizons and possibilities,
        to move out of worn out ways,
For empathy that is stirred
        as experience is shared.
I am glad that we have met,
For I have changed your life
        and you have changed mine.

                                    Jocelyn Grantham[4]

FRIENDSHIP

For the first few months of life, babies are not aware of being separate from their mothers. The realisation of being a distinct entity starts at about six months. Children are terrified by the possibility of abandonment, especially by mother.[5] As they grow in confidence, they naturally seek relationships and friends. The childhood fear of abandonment is replaced by fear of loneliness. It was pointed out in the last chapter that loneliness, while unpleasant, can motivate us to seek out significant friendships.

However, many adults are not good at making close relationships. Friendship is an art to be learned and a skill to be developed. So, what then is friendship? Friendship can be defined as:

A close relationship between two human beings
who enjoy each other's company.

True friendship is characterised by mutual respect, trust, loyalty, love and a desire to share at a deeper level than is possible with most acquaintances. It is like a diamond with many facets, and its various dimensions appeal to different people. Also, as we grow and mature, we appreciate and value different aspects of friendship.

There are varying degrees of friendship. The level of friendship which can be experienced by two people depends on a number of factors: a mutual desire to be friends, opportunities to enjoy their relationship, having common interests, and the level of their communication skills. For a healthy friendship to develop, there also needs to be a high degree of equality in the relationship. While all people are born equal, artificial barriers can get in the way and limit the degree of friendship.

For example, if the social status of two people is very different, their friendship may pose a threat to both of their social groups and could generate opposition from family or other friends. If one person is in a position of authority over the other, it will be hard for them to relate as equals, even if they desire this. The Greek philosopher, Pythagoras, stated: 'Friendship is equality'[6] and down through the centuries equality has been regarded as a basic ingredient of friendship.[7] Augustine called his friend 'thou half of my soul'. Thomas Aquinas defined a friend as an 'alter ego'.

The Relationship Ladder

We all experience different levels of relationship, from people who are total strangers to those who are intimate friends. This whole range of relationships is sometimes called our 'Social Atom'. It is helpful to draw a kind of map to represent the spectrum of relationships in your life, and to identify different categories of relationship: acquaintances, friends, close friends and intimate friends. See exercise (1) at the end of this chapter. Stages of relationship can also be represented progressively, as in the following diagram:

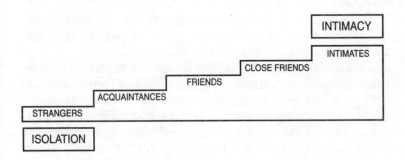

Figure 2. The Relationship Ladder

Most of our contacts in daily life are with *strangers*, especially in urban settings. Large crowds can induce in us a profound sense of loneliness. People often disassociate, or withdraw into themselves in this situation to think their own thoughts and 'do their own thing'. They may not even notice a friend passing in the street. A sad commentary on modern life is the way people can spend half an hour together on a commuter train or bus and not speak to or even acknowledge one another's presence.

The next largest group of people in our lives is *acquaintances* that we meet through work, sport, church and social activities. We may know their names, but have little awareness of their circumstances, let alone their joys or sorrows. The move from being acquainted with someone to friendship is a significant jump. Men tend to have many acquaintances but few personal friends, a lot of 'mates' to whom they may be loyal but not close. They often appear to be content with this. For women the trend is usually reversed, with a smaller circle of acquaintances but more close friends. The results of our survey support this. A greater number of women found it easier to develop friendships than men did; and more men than women stated that they found making friends difficult.

As an introvert, it was not an easy ladder for me (Agnes) to climb. Each step marked a stage in my personal growth. I found it safer to stay on the lower rungs, but this was not satisfying. The right opportunity for friendships came during my nursing training, when I became more confident and found direction in life. I enjoyed rubbing shoulders with other young women who had a similar purpose, as we worked, learned, ate, talked and relaxed together. The friendship of others who shared my Christian faith meant a lot to me. Some of these friendships have lasted over the years, even though our ways have parted. This is because we had a deep involvement in each other's lives, reaching the top step of the ladder at times. Intimacy is scary stuff, but the rewards far outweigh the costs and effort involved.

PRINCIPLES OF FRIENDSHIP

In 1937, Dale Carnegie first published his book *How To Win Friends And Influence People*.[8] At that time, very little literature was available on human relationships, and half a century later this book is still a best seller. Carnegie describes some fundamental principles of relationships, such as listening and not criticising. But his emphasis is more on *influencing people*, rather than making friends. He talks about 'the fine art of influencing people . . . how to win people to your way of thinking . . . fishing for people . . . ways to make people like you . . . how to change people without giving offence'. These skills may be useful in business, but are not part of true friendship. Friends do not use or manipulate one another.

The emphasis of this chapter is on how to develop mutually satisfying friendships without manipulation, having a hidden agenda or using people for personal gain. In a sense we don't *make* friends, we *recognise* them. A friendship is not something to control but to experience and enjoy. As Robert Louis Stevenson said, 'A friend is a gift you give yourself.' But if a friendship is to grow and develop, it needs to be worked at. It requires cultivation and care as much as plants need sunshine and water. This takes time, freely given from both sides. But to develop friends we need more than time, we must have certain attitudes, values and skills.

Attitudes

Our attitudes determine our goals, priorities and behaviour. Attitudes are not in-built but are built-in to our lives; not inherited but learned. The most powerful influence in our lives is the *modelling* we receive from our parents. Our peers and other significant people all affect the development of our attitudes. Cultural values are absorbed often without challenge, primarily via the media. For Christians, biblical values have a compelling influence. But ultimately we all *choose* our attitudes and values and are responsible for them.

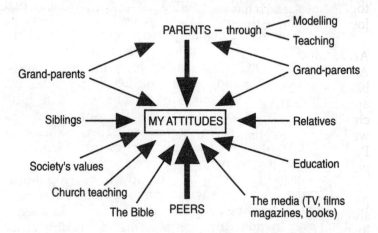

Figure 3. Major factors responsible for our attitudes.

There are a number of attitudes that are necessary for the development of healthy friendships, and four of these are essential:

Love
The word 'friend' comes from the Old English word 'freon' which means to love. The strength of true friendship is love and caring, a desire for the other's good rather than personal advantage. When this attitude is mutual, friendship blossoms. Solomon wrote: 'A friend loves at all times.'[9] Unfortunately, love is a confusing word. It is used to describe a range of emotions, from a passing fancy to a life-long passion; from a selfish desire to possess someone or something to a willingness to lay down my life for a person or cause.

C.S. Lewis made the clear distinction between 'need love' (love which satisfies my desires) and 'gift-love' (unconditional love for the benefit of another).[10] This latter use of the word love is the essence of the Greek word *agape*, which is the main word for love in the New Testament. This kind of loving is the glue that holds friends together. Research has shown that all cultures value selfless love and the loyalty of friends.[11]

Acceptance

Acceptance means to value and receive other people on the basis of *who they are*, not what they do. Most of the love and appreciation that we receive in life has to be earned, both in childhood and as adults. Many people will only accept us if we conform, or change to fit their expectations of us. John Powell says, 'If those who love us will only accept us *in process*, that will be the greatest gift of their love to us.'[12]

Nancy grew up in a home where her well-meaning parents wanted the best for their daughter and hoped that she would be a credit to them. But Nancy felt accepted and loved by them only when she performed well, behaved nicely, kept her room tidy, succeeded at school, and took on their values. Good manners and being seen to do the right thing were more important to her parents than sincerity and caring for others. If she expressed ideas of her own that they did not agree with, a coldness would develop and she would not feel accepted or loved again until she gave in to their ideas. They chose her friends, sports, career and even her clothes.

Nancy did not feel that she had any significance as a person. Naturally, she learned to be critical of others too, and found it hard to accept differences in others. She became a lonely person, desperate for the acceptance she had never received and which she found hard to give.

While this may seem an extreme example, most people that we have talked to about their childhood have experienced mainly conditional love. They felt accepted by their parents on the condition that they performed or achieved according to certain standards. So they continue to try and earn acceptance from others by wearing the right clothes, driving the right make of car, eating the right foods, speaking with the right accent, associating with the right people or living in the right suburb.

It is a rare and beautiful experience to be accepted just for who we are. Paul wrote to the church at Rome, which was composed of many ethnic groups, urging them to 'Accept one another, then, just as Christ accepted you'.[13] Friendships grow best in the soil of mutual acceptance. Acceptance is a powerful proof of love.

Sincerity
'A friend is a person with whom I may be sincere.'[14] This quality of openness and genuineness is also rare. Many people relate most of the time from behind 'masks'. It is not an unusual experience to attend meetings and go away again without really *meeting* anybody. This is because people tend to wear their best masks in public, especially at church.

Friendships grow to the degree that we are prepared to lower our masks, come out from our 'comfort zones', and be real with one another. This means taking the risk of making ourselves vulnerable and exposing our real selves. Of course, being vulnerable to one another can only happen safely after sufficient trust has developed. Samuel Johnson put it this way: 'There can be no friendship without confidence and no confidence without integrity.'

Other-Centredness
In our view, other-centredness is *the most important* attitude that leads to friendship and intimacy. Only when I take the focus off myself and my own needs am I free to see you fully and appreciate you. This liberates me from the prison of my 'world-of-one'. It also communicates to you that you are important to me. The Roman poet, Publius Syrus said: 'We are interested in others when they are interested in us.'

Self-centredness spoils a friendship quicker than anything else. Some people are self-centred because they are basically selfish. Others are self-preoccupied because they do not like themselves, having a poor sense of self-worth. It is not so much a deliberate selfishness, but the ever-present pain of low self-esteem preoccupies their thoughts and energies. Thus they remain inward looking and have nothing left for others.[15] This prevents them from reaching out with genuine interest and concern, and people find relating to them hard work and unrewarding. Quality friendship and intimacy with others are only possible when I have a healthy friendship and intimacy with myself. This is explored further in chapter five.

The ultimate in other-centredness is expressed in the immortal words of Jesus: 'Greater love has no-one than this, that one lay down his life for his friends.'[16] This seldom means literally giving up one's life for others, as Jesus did. For most of us it refers to 'living for', not 'dying for' our friends. Paul defines other-centredness this way: 'Each of you should look not only to your own interests, but also to the interests of others.'[17]

Where it impacts most is in the use of our *time*. A test of true friendship is how much of my time I am prepared to give to you, even when it is inconvenient. Real friends will not begrudge each other time, nor will they take advantage of one another's generosity. A sensitive test of other-centredness is how you react to *interruptions* in your day and respond to intrusions on your time. Our attitudes determine our values in life, and both attitudes and values control behaviour and the quality of friendships.

Values

Friendship as Priority
To have good friends, I have to make friendship a priority and value people more than I value things. If friendships are important to me I will put energy into preserving them. But this takes time and work. 'Friendship is like money, easier made than kept.'[18] The best way to keep friendships from breaking is not to drop them!

I, (John) went to boarding school at seven, in Chefoo,

North China, as my parents were missionaries in Mongolia. Apart from annual holidays, I only spent two full years of my life at home after that. Because I had an open and outgoing nature, I found most people friendly and never felt really lonely. However, I realise now that in response to childhood experiences I became a loner. I enjoyed people but seemed to be able to survive perfectly well without them. As a result, I have had countless acquaintances but realise that I rarely put much energy into developing friendships.

After graduating from medical school, I married someone who became my intimate companion and best friend, and our relationship is mutually satisfying. Our children have become our close friends too, especially as adults. All this made deep friendships with other people seem less necessary. But over recent years, we have both come to realise the value of cultivating friendships, as a couple and individually. We appreciate the input of friends into our lives, because no two people can meet all of each other's social, emotional, intellectual or spiritual needs, however much they love each other.

Loyalty
True friends are people we can trust and rely on, especially in difficult times. You soon discover who your real friends are when a crisis occurs and you need help. Solomon made some shrewd observations about this:

> Wealth brings many friends,
>   but a poor man's friend deserts him . . .
> Many curry favour with a ruler,
>   and everyone is the friend of a man who gives gifts.
> A poor man is shunned by all his relatives —
>   how much more do his friends avoid him!
> Though he pursues them with pleading,
>   they are nowhere to be found.[19]

One important aspect of loyalty is *confidentiality*. This does not mean being secretive about your friends, but careful not to share their confidences with others. This applies sometimes even to sharing information with your spouse. Many friendships have been spoiled in church fellowships, where confidences have been shared too freely. A survey was done in 1979 by *Psychology Today* on over 40,000 people to determine the qualities of friendship that people considered were important.[20] At the head of the list were 'Keeping confidences' (89%) and 'Loyalty' (88%).

Information travels fast on the human 'grape vine'. Gossip is a common cause of conflict in families and among friends. Mark Twain once said, 'May God defend me from my friends!'

> If you love someone you will always be loyal to him/her no matter what the cost. You will always believe in him/her, always expect the best of him/her, always stand your ground in defending him/her.[21]

Fun and Challenge
Friendship is one of the joys of living. Good friendships should be both enjoyable and stimulating. One test of the quality of a friendship is whether you are a better person after being in the company of your friend. Friends should stimulate one another to grow emotionally, intellectually and spiritually. 'People learn from one another, just as iron sharpens iron.'[22]

A friend can also provide valuable feedback, insights, and a challenge to personal growth. A trusted friend will help me discover my 'blind spots', or 'bad breath' areas, if our relationship is built on honesty. An old Jewish proverb puts it this way: 'A friend is someone who warns you.' In a healthy relationship, friends are mutually accountable. We can help each other to grow in personal awareness, maturity, integrity and spirituality.

Friendships based on the above attitudes and values are priceless. They change relationships from black-and-white to colour. They enrich life and dispel loneliness. 'They redouble joys and cut grief in half. . . . Those who lack friends to open themselves to are cannibals of their own hearts.'[23]

The Third Party
We are convinced from our own experience that there is one more dimension that is necessary to a fully rounded friendship. This is when God is part of it, the third partner in the relationship. This applies to all deep friendships, including marriage. Three thousand years ago, the writer of Ecclesiastes painted a word picture which is up to date in its description of friendship, compared with loneliness:

> I also observed another piece of foolishness around the earth. This is the case of a man who is quite alone, without a son or brother, yet he works hard to keep gaining more riches, and to whom will he leave it all? And why is he giving up so much now? It is all so pointless and depressing.
>
> *Two* can accomplish more than twice as much as one, for the results can be much better. If one falls, the other pulls him up; but if a man falls when he is alone, he's in trouble . . .
>
> And one standing alone can be attacked and defeated, but two can stand back-to-back and conquer; *Three* is even better, for a triple-braided cord is not easily broken.[24]

The lonely man described here seemed to have put more energy into acquiring wealth than developing friendships, even with family. This scenario is played out many times in our materialistic culture. A rope made of three braided strands is a perfect metaphor for the relationship of two friends and God. Braiding strands of cord together increases the tensile strength of the rope. When stress is applied to the ends, the immediate effect is to draw the strands closer together. A triple-braided cord, two friends and God, is an unbreakable combination.

Figure 4. 'A triple-braided cord is not easily broken'

We are all born with the capacity and desire to relate and form friendships but without the skills to do so. If we do not see these modelled for us in our formative years, we will have to learn them as adults. Having the above attitudes and values increases our desire to develop the skills.

FRIENDSHIP SKILLS

The quality of a relationship between friends depends on the effectiveness of their communication. Solomon said: 'An unreliable messenger can cause a lot of trouble. Reliable communication permits progress.'[25] The following is a brief description of the essentials of good communication.

Creative Listening
The foundation of good communication between two people is listening. Listening sounds easy, but it is in fact hard work. To listen to you, I must temporarily set aside my own world of thoughts and emotions and focus my attention on you. I must leave where I am to go to where you are, to sit in your seat, to walk in your shoes for a while. Good listeners are rare. This is because few of us have been listened to as we were growing up, and also because we would rather talk than listen.

We all have two ears and one mouth, but have an urge to

reverse the ratio! While someone is talking, our minds are often thinking about something else, often what we want to say next rather than what is being said. Paul Tournier called this process 'the dialogue of the deaf'. This is nothing new. James wrote long ago: 'Everyone should be quick to listen, slow to speak.'[26]

Listening is healing. Listening is loving. Paul Tillich said: 'The first duty of love is to listen.' Listening is being other-centred. In listening I am trying to understand who *you are*, as well as what you say. 'At the heart of creative listening is the understanding that we are, in partnership, participating in a process.'[27] When you listen to me, trying to understand me and what I am saying, I understand myself better. Creative listening is active, not passive, learning to grasp the 'inner consistency of others'.[28] This is the foundation of intimacy: two people who know and understand each other.

Feedback

Listening and really hearing one another is only half the process of active listening. The other skill to be mastered is the art of giving appropriate feed-back. When a message is given, the sender needs to know whether the receiver has understood the message correctly. The message may be encoded in spoken words, non-verbal body language or writing. As the message is de-coded by the receiver, it always passes through a *'filter'* which alters the message.

Parts of the message, especially what the receiver does not want to hear or does not understand, are filtered out. Other things will be added in, depending on the emotional state, beliefs, prejudices or past experiences of the receiver. The filtering process is mostly unconscious, though sometimes is deliberate. So, I can never tell you what you have said, *I can only tell you what I have heard.* What I hear is what you have said minus what I have filtered out, plus what I have added in. The communication process is summarised in Figure 5.

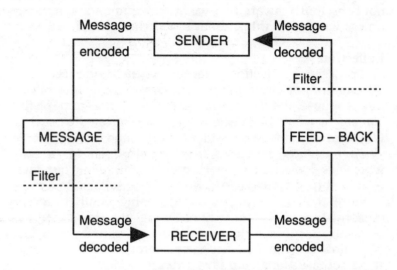

Figure 5. The Communication Process

The message received may be similar to the one that was
sent, but is usually an interpretation of it, and sometimes
can be very different. For example, a wife says to her
husband as he comes in: 'You're rather late tonight.' His
response will depend on the filter in his mind that her
message passed through, such as: 'She's checking up on
me again'; 'She's upset'; 'I wish she wouldn't fuss over me
like my mother did'; 'My wife really cares about me and
was worrying in case I'd had an accident'. There are other
possibilities.

If he just grunts, or does not reply, they are both left
guessing. It may take two or three times around the cycle
just described before the message received fully agrees with
the message sent. If the message received is unclear, the
receiver either has to take steps to clarify it or else operate on
an assumption, which is a risk. Assumptions are damaging
to relationships because there is at least a fifty per cent

chance that they will be wrong. That degree of failure is not good enough for healthy friendships. But so often we are not consciously aware that we are making an assumption, unless we stop to think about it and check it out.

Reflection

The process of reflection is far more than giving feedback, information, or clarifying misunderstandings. 'In a reflective response, the listener re-states the feelings and/or the content of what the speaker has communicated in such a way that demonstrates understanding and acceptance.'[29] Good reflection expresses true empathy. This is a skill which we have had to work hard to master in our own relationship as well as in our work as counsellors. Reflection is more than re-stating or paraphrasing what the other person has said. It is a way of telling you that I can see, or am trying to see the world through your eyes. It lets you know whether I have clearly heard, or not heard, both what you are *saying* and how you are *feeling*.

This is different from the glib statement, 'I know how you feel.' Nobody can really know how another person feels.[30] But by accurate reflection I can communicate to you that I am beginning to understand what it is like to be you. When someone does that for me, I feel loved and accepted, no longer alone in the world. This is a priceless gift that two friends can give each other.

The skills of good communication can be learned at any stage in life. One young man was a social disaster in his early years. He was good with an axe but not with words. At twenty-eight he asked a woman to marry him, and then added, 'My opinion is that you had better not do it.' She took his advice! Later he became a successful lawyer and mastered the art of communication, oratory and debate. In 1860 he was elected to be the sixteenth President of the United States, Abraham Lincoln.

Self-Revelation

If empathy and reflection are ways of letting you know that

I understand you, self-revelation opens the door so that you can *understand me*. Essentially, it means revealing my feelings, and I am not going to do that except with friends I trust. But I will never be able to develop close friendships without sharing my real self. Sharing feelings is not easy. It is scary, because it makes us vulnerable.

Because I (John) had become a loner at an early age, I seldom shared my feelings with others. I absorbed the message, 'big boys don't cry', and that revealing feelings was a sign of weakness, especially for males. I also learned from my Christian sub-culture that feelings were suspect and unreliable. This meant that I was not only expected to hide my feelings, but I should not even have them, at least not the negative ones!

One of the biggest discoveries of my life has been that feelings are valid, neither good nor bad, and are the essence of who I am. I cannot ignore them and remain healthy, but I can control them and use them constructively. If someone wants to really know me, he or she needs to know my feelings, and if we want to grow in our friendship and intimacy, the process has to be mutual. This discovery transformed our marriage from a good one into a great one. The *process* of self-revelation is explored further in chapter seven.

Summary

We have defined briefly the meaning of friendship. It is a bit like trying to describe a rainbow to a visually-impaired person, or snow to someone who lives in the tropics. Most people desire rewarding relationships but have few deep friendships. The ability to have close and meaningful friendships depends on our attitudes, values and communication skills. If I feel lonely and friendless, I can change. To have a friend I must be a friend: emerge from my world-of-one and become other-centred.

REFLECTIONS AND EXERCISES

1. SOCIAL ATOM   One way of defining your 'social atom' is to draw three concentric circles on a large sheet of paper.

   - In the *centre* write names of people you consider are close or intimate friends.
   - In the *middle* circle write names of people who are good friends: people you might visit, invite for a meal, or like talking to.
   - In the *outer* circle write names (or initials) of people who are casual acquaintances. These are people you know and may talk to occasionally, but are not a significant part of your life.

   • Underline the names of those friends, particularly those in the inner and middle circles, who do not live nearby, which means that you do not have regular contact.
   • If you have moved or plan to move (e.g. for retirement), how would this affect your 'social atom'?
   • Are you satisfied with the number of people included in the inner and middle circles?
   • Discuss the implications of your social atom with your group.

2. FRIENDSHIP   Write down all the qualities you would look for in a friend.

   • Are these what you offer in your friendship with others?
   • Ask a close friend what qualities she/he values in you.
   • Would you choose yourself as a friend? If not, why not?
   • Reflect on these questions in your journal and discuss them together in your group.

3. UNCONDITIONAL LOVE AND ACCEPTANCE   Think back to your childhood.

- How much unconditional love did you receive from your family or friends?
- How much of the love and acceptance you received at home or at school do you think was because of achievement, and how much was just for being you? Did you have to earn acceptance?

4. OTHER-CENTREDNESS How other-centred do you think you are? Some indicators could be:

   - The amount of time you give to others.
   - How annoyed you become with interruptions, such as people wanting your time when you are busy.
   - How often you contact friends by letter or phone.
   - How much you pray for others.

5. LISTENING Assess your listening skills using this simple exercise. Pair up with someone and choose a subject to discuss. One person makes a statement and finishes with the words: 'What do you hear me saying?' The other person paraphrases what was said to the satisfaction of the speaker before continuing the conversation. She/he can then reply to the first statement, also finishing with the words, 'What do you hear me saying?'

   - Continue this interchange for a while and observe how accurate you are in both giving and receiving messages.

6. EYE CONTACT
   a) Have a serious conversation with someone for two or three minutes, facing each other with good eye contact.
   b) Then have a similar conversation, sitting back-to-back, so that you cannot see each other.

      - What differences did you observe in:
        - your level of comfort or discomfort,
        - the amount of information you missed the second time round, particularly subtle inferences,

– your enthusiasm for the conversation.

7. A GROUP EXERCISE IN SELF-REVELATION   Find an object in your house or garden with which you can identify: perhaps an ornament, flower, picture or any other item. Think about how this represents you in some way, and what it says about your goals or dreams.

- Share this with a friend, or in your group. (Agree to make this conversation completely confidential.) Make no evaluative comments about what each says. Ask clarifying questions only, or just make reflections which convey that you understand. Be as open as you can about yourself.
- If you do not have a friend that you want to share this with, spend some time writing your thoughts in your journal.

THREE

INTIMACY

This is my lover, this is my friend.
                              Song of Songs[1]

I ntimacy builds on friendship, and an intimate relationship usually includes the attitudes, values and skills
described in the last chapter. The progression of friendship
into deeper intimacy depends on the degree of *self-revelation*
that takes place in the relationship.

DEFINITIONS OF INTIMACY

The word intimacy comes from the Latin, *intima*, meaning
inner or innermost. The real person inside is often different
from the persona that is projected to others.[2] Intimacy is
commonly thought of in the context of sexual activity,
but it has a much broader meaning, which does not
necessarily include sex. Someone has described intimacy
succinctly as: 'INTO ME SEE' – two people seeing past
each other's 'masks' and making contact with the real
person.

Each of us has our own sense of inner personal space, and
intimacy happens when two people combine their personal
spaces to enjoy a shared space. I can experience true
intimacy when I am able to be myself fully in the presence
of another.[3] We all guard our personal space, because we
have all been hurt to some extent in childhood and have
learned protective mechanisms. These are like walls that
we build around us.

We all live in our own 'castles', and for some the walls
are very thick. But every castle has a drawbridge, which
is controlled on the inside. So each of us can let it down
to allow someone in if we wish. When two people start
to build a level of trust between them, it is like lowering
their drawbridges a little to one another. If it looks safe,
they will lower them further until eventually they are
able to walk across and meet each other.[4] They can now
experience intimacy, which we define as:

> *A relationship where two people strive*
> *to know and be known.*

For you to know me fully, I need to be willing and able to
reveal myself to you. If I do not like myself, or am afraid of
rejection, I will fail to show you who I really am. Also, if I
do not have the communication skills to reveal my feelings
and my inner self, you will never know me.

For me to know you to that degree, I have to be other-
centred rather than self-focussed. True intimacy can only
develop where there is a mutual desire for self-revelation.
Erik Erickson describes this quality of intimacy in his
definition of love: 'The mutuality of mates and partners is a shared identity . . . through an experience of
finding oneself in another.'[5] Stephanie Dowrick expands
this picture further: 'Being really myself in the presence of
another; allowing someone else to be true to who they are
in my presence. No one in control and no one struggling for
control; unconditional love, acceptance, closeness, trust, no
masks.'[6]

This kind of relationship, based on respect and love,
allows each to grow to their potential in a wholesome way
and freely give of themselves to each other. Real intimacy
is the deepest expression of love, originating from a desire
to give rather than take. Reis defined the development of
intimacy more precisely:

The intimacy process begins when one person expresses,

through verbal or nonverbal means, personally revealing feelings or information to another person. It
continues when the listener responds empathetically.
For an interaction to become intimate, the discloser
must feel understood, validated, and cared for by
the listener. Both participant's behaviour depend on
the other's behaviour and response, as well as their
own pre-existing or situationally determined motives,
needs, and goals.[7]

DIMENSIONS OF INTIMACY

Just as friendship has many facets, so does intimacy. The
following are a few descriptions of intimacy by various
respondents in our survey.

- Total, mutual, voluntary sharing between two people.
  (Male / 36)
- Closeness with another person physically, intellectu-
  ally, emotionally and spiritually. (Female / 28)
- A mutual, uninhibited sharing, with respect and
  understanding. (Male / 42)
- An open, caring relationship that allows freedom for
  each person to be him/herself. (Female / 27)
- A shared closeness which includes each other's con-
  cerns, hopes, dreams, joys and sorrows. (Female /
  24)
- An unconditional expression of love and respect
  for each other as unique and worthy individuals.
  (Male / 26)
- A relationship where all ideas and feelings are shared.
  (Male / 39)

The 300 respondents in our survey were asked the open
question: 'How would you define intimacy?' The main concepts expressed in their answers were analysed:

FACTOR	PERCENTAGE		FACTOR	PERCENTAGE	
Gender	Male	Female		Male	Female
Numbers	104	196		104	196
Sharing feelings	50 .0	47.4	Shared spirituality	4.8	10.3
Closeness	31.7	32.5	Total honesty	4.8	9.8
Touch	15.4	23.7	Mutual respect	3.8	8.2
Mutual trust	17.3	21.6	Absence of fear	6.7	6.7
Total sharing	19.2	19.1	Shared ideas	8.7	5.2
Acceptance	20.2	18.0	Shared experiences	4.8	6.2
Good communication	13.5	18.0	Shared dreams	3.8	6.7
Able to be self	10.6	11.3	Love	3.8	6.7
Vulnerability	8.7	8.8	Mutual caring	4.8	5.7

Figure 6. Qualities of intimacy identified in survey

Sharing feelings was by far the most significant factor identified as essential for intimacy by both men and women. Although approximately the same proportion of men and women referred to this, men are usually not so good at sharing feelings. This is probably the reason more women emphasised the need for good communication. It is interesting that mutual trust, acceptance, honesty and respect were higher on the list than love. The ability to be yourself stands out, and is balanced by the importance of being vulnerable to one another. More women commented on the importance to them both of sharing at a *spiritual* level, and honesty in the relationship.

Intimacy can be experienced in five major ways: physical touch; emotional sharing; intellectual interaction; social activity and spiritual communication. Respondents to our survey were asked to rate the importance to them of these five aspects of intimacy in the following categories:

- vital
- very important
- moderately important
- nice if it happens
- not important.

After combining their answers to Vital and Very Important, the results are shown in Figure 7.

Emotional intimacy was very important to ninety-four per cent of all respondents, with no difference in the emphasis placed on this by men or women. A noticeable gender difference as we already remarked was in *spiritual* communication, where more women than men thought this was vital or very important to intimacy (F: 88% / M: 78%). This difference also showed up in the definition of intimacy, analysed in Figure 6.

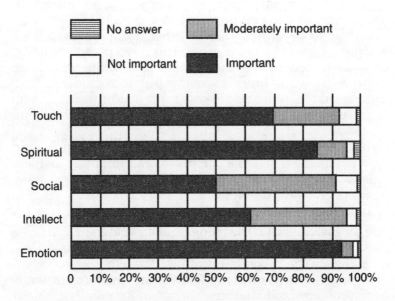

Figure 7. The importance of the five main ways of expressing intimacy for 300 people.

INTIMACY IN MARRIAGE

Marriage provides a relationship in which intimacy has the best opportunity to flourish. Unfortunately, this is not so for many couples who experience living-together-loneliness (described in chapter one). Sixty-two per cent of married people in our survey claimed they felt lonely at times in their relationship. In response to another question, sixty-three per cent of single people claimed that they experience loneliness daily or sometimes.

The main reasons given for loneliness in marriage were poor communication, busyness, conflicting needs and unresolved conflict. For others, the loneliness is not so intense, but they do not have the intimacy that one or other, or both of them really desire. They may not be able to articulate their problem, but feel a vague dissatisfaction in their relationship, a longing that has not been met.

Of the 222 married people in our survey, a quarter of them expressed the opinion that they expected intimacy in marriage to be greater than in other relationships, a total sharing of life. Sharing feelings, trust, acceptance, honesty and a reciprocal experience of love and caring were high on the list. Four times as many people considered that their need for intimacy differed from that of their partner, compared with those who regarded their needs to be about the same.

Just over three-quarters of the married group in our survey claimed that the quality of the intimacy in their relationships had improved over the years. The main reasons given for this were:

- a growing understanding of one another
- a strong commitment to their relationship growth
- the ability to communicate well
- shared experiences in life, especially working through problems and conflict
- the development of trust in their relationship
- a shared faith.

Some people claimed that intimacy in their relationship had decreased. The reasons they gave were similar to those listed above by people experiencing loneliness in their marriage.

INTIMACY WITHOUT FRIENDSHIP

There are certain situations where people can experience significant degrees of intimacy without having had a prior friendship. A friendship may or may not develop between the two people afterwards. Some examples of this are:

Professional Relationships
In the helping professions, honest sharing and self-revelation has to take place for there to be any benefit. But this does not usually happen in *both* directions, as it would in a friendship. The client may reveal a lot to a counsellor, psychotherapist, doctor, social worker, lawyer, accountant, spiritual director or priest, but it is usually inappropriate for the helping professional to share at that level in return. However, real intimacy has been experienced between the two people, which could be very significant for both, even though it was not an equal sharing.

Books
Books provide another source of intimacy without actual friendship in the flesh. We can name a number of authors whom we feel close to, because we share their ideals and values. We have enjoyed meeting and developing a relationship with a few of them. But whether or not you meet the authors, in reading their writings it is possible to share their thoughts and emotions, which is the essence of intimacy.

Small Group Situations
These can provide significant degrees of intimacy even where prior friendships may not exist. There can be a high degree of intimate revelation by people in small group

settings, such as a church home group, a growth or study group, an intense learning situation, a seminar or religious meeting.

We have run Marriage Enrichment Seminars regularly for twenty years, with a total attendance of about 2000 couples. We observed much intimacy in these groups because people often shared at a heart level. Some participants developed close friendships afterwards. We also noticed that an openness and deep sharing often took place more quickly in groups of people who were total *strangers*, than in groups where people already knew each other.

Analysis of our survey data seems to show that small group experience helps people to be better at making friends. (Significant to a 90% confidence level. See Figure 8.) It could be argued that people with an outgoing personality, or those who have already developed good communication skills, are better at making friends and also would be attracted to small groups. However, our observations in many small group situations would suggest that they contained a higher proportion of introverts to extroverts than occurs in the general population. We conclude that participation in small groups assists people to learn the skills needed for friendship and intimacy.

Eighty-four per cent of the respondents in our survey were currently part of a small group or had been in the past. Much the same proportion of men and women attended groups (M= 82%; F= 85%). The commonest type of small group experienced was a church Bible study or a home group. Others were growth and awareness groups (including Marriage Enrichment, Marriage Encounter and Twelve-step groups); groups for therapy, supervision, or emotional support; work team groups; friendship groups; common interest groups (such as parenting or book reading).

The attitudes, values and communication skills already defined need to be operating for intimacy to be experienced in a small group. There must be acceptance, trust, sincerity, love and other-centredness, as well as creative listening and

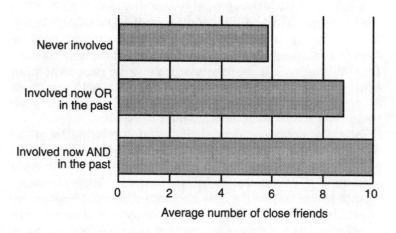

Figure 8. Relationship between small group attendance and
number of friends.

self-revelation in action. These skills can be modelled and
learned in a well-run small group.

Unfortunately, these qualities are often missing in church
settings, even in home groups. Over a third of respondents
in our survey who attend church said that they experienced
little or no real intimacy through their church fellowships,
even though they may have been part of a home group. For
further comment on the value of small groups and how to
run them see chapter five.

RISKS OF INTIMACY

Many people have a longing for intimacy in their lives and
can be greatly affected by the experience of intimacy in
one of the situations described above. For example, in a
counselling or pastoral care context, where the client has
self-disclosed, we have sometimes been deeply influenced

by this. Conversely, clients can be profoundly affected by receiving such caring, listening, acceptance, and unconditional love. They may never have experienced anything like this before. This is good for them.

But there is a danger that professional relationships, which start in a healthy way, can lead to emotional or even sexual involvement, with untold hurt for both parties. This highlights the necessity for those in people-helping professions to have proper supervision. Part of the purpose of supervision is to help the therapist deal with such transference and counter-transference issues.

Intimacy is powerful medicine, and is missing from the lives of many people. When it is experienced in small groups, for example in a growth group or a learning situation, it can have disturbing effects. Michelle came from a home where there was little intimacy. Her parents never shared their feelings, and conversations at home were superficial. At eighteen she enrolled at a Bible School. After a few weeks, the group of thirty students began to trust one another and become more open. In discussion times among the students, Mark often expressed his ideas, including doubts and feelings. He made himself vulnerable in a way Michelle had never observed before in a man.

After a while, she felt she really knew him as a person, and was attracted to him. She began to have romantic fantasies about him, including marriage. The problem was that this possibility had not occurred to Mark! He seldom noticed Michelle, who interpreted this as rejection, and then went out of her way to avoid him. She was responding to the experience of intimacy in the group, but was not mature enough to evaluate what was happening to her.

Both these examples illustrate the importance of establishing clear 'boundaries' in our lives. We need to define where our boundaries begin and end in all our relationships. This helps to prevent inappropriate invasion of another's personal space, and also the misinterpretation of expressions of intimacy encountered with our family,

friends and colleagues. Defining clear but not rigid boundaries in our relationships is part of maturity.

PERSONAL HISTORY

Modelling

Intimacy skills are learned. The model that we observed
while growing up is the most powerful determining factor
in our ability to be intimate. Many values and attitudes
derived from our parents may be good and consistent with
healthy relationships. We can reaffirm these. But *all aspects*
of our background need careful and honest assessment.
If we identify some attitudes that are detrimental to our
ability to experience intimacy, they can be challenged and
replaced.

Figure 9 shows the experience of the people in our
intimacy survey in terms of closeness to their immediate
family. A greater number of people reported that they had
been closer to mother than father. Closeness to brothers and
sisters was about equal. The much smaller number who
were close to their grandparents, and the high number
who had no answer to this question, reflect the fact that
many of them had little or no contact with grandparents.
The differences in the experience of women and men is
shown in Figure 10.

Experiencing closeness to parents and siblings affects the
quality of later relationships. Respondents who claimed to
have been close or very close to their parents found it
easier to make friends in later life than those who had
a somewhat distant relationship with parents. A similar
trend was seen for those who had been close to or distant
from their siblings.

Another measure of the effect of modelling showed up
in people's experience of intimacy in marriage in later life.
Those who had observed intimacy in their parents' and sib-
ling's relationships were much more likely to have regular
or daily significant conversations with their partners than
those who had not.

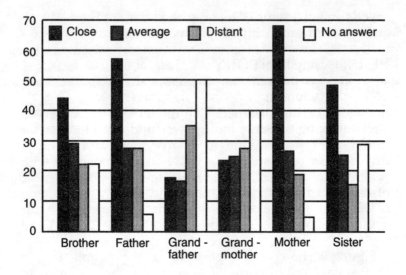

Figure 9. Experience of intimacy in family of origin

Culture
Social Norms
There are a number of historical and cultural factors which affect our desire for intimacy and ease in forming intimate relationships. These are explored more fully in the next chapter. They include such things as attitudes to material possessions, individualism, achievement and gender issues. While home is the primary influence which determines our ability to be intimate, we are also strongly affected by peers and the subtle pressures of our culture.

Christian Faith
The Bible stresses the importance of relationships, commitment, good communication, love, respect and other-centredness. These are all necessary ingredients of intimacy. An honest application of this teaching must influence the quality of relationships. Many respondents in our survey said that church attendance provided opportunity for friendships.

Even though a third of those who identified themselves as members of a church claimed that this seldom provided for them experiences of intimacy, many referred to their faith as an important factor in their ability to be intimate. Fifty-five per cent claimed that a shared faith either improved relationships or was vital to true intimacy. Others commented on how it gave them much more in common, a foundation on which to build, enabling them to share at all levels.

Personal Growth

Individuals differ not only in their family background, culture and faith, but also in the degree to which they have matured. Many people have limited self-awareness and spend little time attending to their emotional, social and spiritual growth. In chapter five we focus on the importance of knowing yourself and developing intimacy with yourself. This is a pre-requisite to intimacy with others. Chapter six looks at some internal blocks that can prevent intimacy, however much we may desire it. Then in chapter seven we identify important keys to intimacy, all related to personal growth and maturity.

INTIMACY FOR MEN

Male Friendships

Many stories have been recorded down through the ages about close and enduring friendships between men. Perhaps the best known is that of David the shepherd and Jonathan, prince of Israel. 'Jonathan became one in spirit with David, and he loved him as himself.'[8] This love overrode political and family loyalties and remained unchanged until they were parted by death.

A thousand years later, Jesus and his disciples modelled intimacy between men. (Jesus also had close relationships

with women.) In particular, we know that Jesus and John
had an intimate friendship, and John refers to himself a
number of times as 'the disciple whom Jesus loved'.[9] The
kind of love between Jesus and his disciples is intended to
unite all Christians.[10]

Examples of intimacy between males in ancient Greek
literature abound: Achilles and Patroclus, Pylades and
Orestes, Amys and Amylion, to name a few. Homer's
epics depict a deep and lasting love bond between men.[11]
In feudal times, special ties bound a man and his male
'companion', who may have been fostered into the same
family. Their friendship even overshadowed ties binding
blood relatives.[12] In British mythology, stories like those
of King Arthur and the knights of the Round Table, Robin
Hood and his merry outlaws describe male friendships
which stayed true through thick and thin. Close male
friendship has been observed by anthropologists in many
societies today.[13]

Clearly, men have always been regarded as capable of
intimacy, and male friendship of this kind has sometimes been spoken of as being stronger than marriage.
Only recently has it been assumed that close relationships
between men (or between women) will inevitably be homosexual in nature. Homosexual relationships are common
today, and are more openly expressed than previously.
Some of them are lasting, strong friendships, but most
'gay' relationships tend to be transitory. Many heterosexual men are afraid of developing close relationships
with other men for fear of being labelled 'gay'. Sometimes
they fear that they might even become homosexual as a
result.[14]

Herein lies a dilemma. Because we are sexual beings, we
cannot relate to others asexually, yet feelings of tenderness
between people are not sexual as such. But if men do not
know what to do with these feelings, they ignore them and
often lose out on close friendships with other men. This
is unfortunate, because men are greatly enriched through
deep friendships with one another. Roy McCloughry in his

book *Men and Masculinity* writes powerfully of the value of close male friendships.[15]

Men in Groups

Anthropologists studying male bonding behaviour find that men have a socio-biological propensity to relate in groups. It is suggested that this started with pre-historic man specialised in hunting in all-male groups.[16] Sport is regarded as the modern equivalent of hunting, and male bonding is the central organising feature of sport. The most popular male team sports involve a degree of aggression. Sociologists claim that many sports are a form of preparation for war. 'The battle of Waterloo was won on the playing fields of Eton.'[17] War is certainly almost universally a male enterprise.

Secret societies have always been attractive to men. Well-known ones are Freemasons, Orangemen, Ku Klux Klan, Mafia, Carboroni and Black Muslims. The Nazis were predominately a male organisation. Attraction to secret societies probably expresses a need to be a man-among-men, as much as political or social unrest. All-male clubs and particularly all-male drinking venues have been popular for centuries though these bastions of maleness have been challenged recently by women.

Many wives fear their husbands congregating in all-male groups, especially secret ones. There may be a number of reasons for this, but at the very least, this behaviour limits opportunities for family intimacy. Men's service groups have become increasingly popular this century, such as Rotary and Lions clubs. These are some ways that men use to try and compensate for lack of intimacy in their lives.

Men and Women

Intimate relationships between men and women have been described traditionally in romantic terms, rather than emphasizing other important aspects of intimacy. Until recently, little was written about close friendships

and companionship between men and women. We believe
that the potential for intimacy across the genders is just as
great, or greater, than within gender groups.

In our work with couples, we frequently talk to people
who say that they experience little true intimacy in their
marriages. Usually it is the wife who complains of this
lack. Husbands sometimes say that they don't even know
what she is talking about! This is not because men are
less capable of sharing intimately, but because they have
been conditioned out of it. One psychologist has called this
'trained incompetence'.[18] In chapter seven we explore in
more depth the skill of feelings-sharing and also reasons
why men find this difficult.

Researchers have shown that 'both sexes have a biologically based need for intimacy'.[19] Our survey results show
that male respondents defined intimacy in the same wholistic terms as females did. Men also stated that they desired
much the same degree of intimacy in marriage as women
wanted. However, fifty per cent of married women stated
that their partners were less interested in sharing feelings
than they were, and only fourteen per cent of husbands
commented on this. There seems to be a gap between the
desire that men have for closeness in relationships with
women and their actual experience of intimacy together,
particularly in terms of sharing feelings.

INTIMACY FOR WOMEN

There are fewer stories in literature describing close friendships between women than there are about men. Maybe this
is because most writers until fairly recently were men! The
beautiful story of Ruth and her mother-in-law Naomi is an
exception, which crosses the boundaries of age, family and
race. Ruth said: 'Don't make me leave you, for I want to
go wherever you go, and to live wherever you live; your
people shall be my people, and your God shall be my God;
I want to die where you die, and be buried there.'[20]

Close relationships between mothers and their daughters

are generally more common than between fathers and their sons. Some sons are very close to their mothers. This can be healthy, but it sometimes represents a failure to establish proper independence. Figure 10 shows the percentages of men and women in our survey who claimed to have had a close (or very close) relationship with parents, grandparents and siblings.

CLOSE RELATIONSHIP	MEN	WOMEN
with mother	57%	55%
with father	40	41
with sister	34	40
with brother	34	28
with grandfather	15	24
with grandmother	24	15

Figure 10. Close relationships in families

These results show that both men and women are more likely to have a closer relationship with mothers than with fathers. It appears that men had a closer relationship with their grandmothers and women with grandfathers. The figures suggest that friendships between sisters are more likely to be stronger than that between sisters and brothers. Unmarried sisters will often live together and may share a business together. This may be part of the reason why women are more likely than men to form groups for specific interests or just to socialise. Researchers have observed that women use groups more for intimate social interaction than men do.

LANGUAGE AND INTIMACY

A lot of research has been done on ways men and women use language, and this gives strong evidence to support the contention that women are more concerned with intimacy than men. This is explained superbly in a book by Deborah Tannen: *You Just Don't Understand*.[21] Her contention is not only that men and women use language differently, but that understanding 'genderlect' will improve communication and increase our ability to accept one another.

She shows how men view the world in a hierarchical social order, seeing themselves either as one-up or one-down in comparison with others. Life for men is a contest to preserve independence, and talk is for *information*. On the other hand, women mostly use conversations to negotiate intimacy and talk is mainly for *interaction*. Numerous studies of children at play show that these differences appear to be gender conditioned. Boys often play in large groups, hierarchically structured and usually with a leader who likes to give orders. In their games there are always winners and losers. Girls often play in small groups or pairs. For them, differentiation is measured by closeness, especially to the popular girl. Girls are more concerned with being liked than with status.

Tannen points out that in communication, the key for men is *independence*, but for women is *inter-dependence* and intimacy. They are more concerned with community. Men want to know: 'Do you respect me?' and women: 'Do you like me?'. Men prefer to use what Tannen calls 'Report-talk', and women prefer 'Rapport-talk'. Men talk a lot in public but are often silent at home, whereas it is usually the reverse with women. When men tell stories they usually include themselves and what they did, whereas women usually talk about other people. Male-only talk is often about work or sport, and female-only conversations are about people.

For men, interrupting a conversation shows involvement, and argument means interraction. For women, interruption is generally regarded as rudeness and agreement is evidence of intimacy, whether they fully agree with the speaker or not! Men are less likely than women to ask for information, because that 'frames' them as inferior to the person with the information. Many arguments have been triggered between couples when husbands have got lost while driving because they refused to ask for directions! Men see their friends as people to *do things with*. Women see friends primarily as people with whom *to talk*.

TOWARDS INTIMACY BETWEEN THE SEXES

The observations just made are not all desirable behaviours, but they are certainly true to life. They reveal a lot about the relative inclination that men and women have towards intimacy. But our gender conditioning is *not who we are*. What we have learned can be un-learned or modified. When men and women understand each other better it makes a good start towards better relationships and intimacy.

We need more than understanding. Intimacy is hard enough between people of the same gender who do have some awareness about how each other thinks and feels. The problem has been humorously defined as 'Men are from Mars and women from Venus!'[22] We are different, but these differences can be combined to form intimate relationships with infinite variety. How to understand ourselves and develop intimate relationships with other people is what the rest of this book is about.

Summary

Intimacy is a wonderful but illusive experience. It is deeply desired and yet seems out of reach for many people. Ability to form intimate relationships is affected by our gender, the model we have observed in our family of origin and our background. It is also influenced by how much self-awareness we have and our level of personal growth and maturity. There is clear evidence to suggest that men and women differ in their ability to experience intimacy. But we can learn from each other, and can all learn to develop intimacy skills.

REFLECTIONS AND EXERCISES

1. INTIMACY   Write down your definition of intimacy.
   Explore as many facets of intimacy as you can. How
   much of your definition expresses your actual experience
   of intimacy, and how much reflects what you would like
   but may not have known in the past? From whom did
   you learn about intimacy?

   • Share your definition and thoughts in your small
     group. List aspects of intimacy that you all have
     in common, and those that are unique to different
     individuals.
   • Try to come up with a core definition of intimacy with
     which all members of the group can identify.

2. INTIMACY IN MARRIAGE

   • If you are married, in what ways does your intimacy
     together differ from intimacy you experience with
     others?
   • Are you both comfortable and satisfied with the
     quality of intimacy that you have in your marriage?
     Discuss ways in which you might grow in your inti-
     macy. See the exercises at the end of chapter nine.

3. SMALL GROUPS   Do you belong to a small group of
   any kind?

   • If so, does it provide opportunities for intimacy?
   • How could these be improved?
   • If you do not belong to a small group, are you
     interested in joining one, or even starting one? (For
     ideas on Growth Groups see chapter five.)

4. RISKS OF INTIMACY   If you are in a one-on-one
   people-helping situation, do you have a supervisor? If
   not, it would be worth finding one.

   • If you are receiving counselling, does your counsellor

or therapist have supervision? If you are looking for a counsellor, it is wise to make sure that the person you choose is supervised.

5. YOUR MODELLING   A valuable learning experience is to reflect on your modelling. This is not a blaming exercise. Most parents did the best they knew how in the difficult task of bringing up children.

Reflect in your journal on the following questions:

- What expressions of intimacy, verbally or physically, did you observe in your parents' interaction?
- How close did you personally feel to your mother and father?
- Did your parents talk about their feelings with each other in front of you, or with you? Did they process their feelings, or just act them out? Did they *tell you* they loved you?
- Did your parents relate their faith to everyday life?
- What were their attitudes to money, work, leisure, pleasure, sex, religion, parenting, entertaining, people of other ethnic groups? To what extent do you think their attitudes have influenced yours?

If you are married, it would be a helpful learning experience to share together your answers to these questions.

6. GENDER ISSUES   What experience do you have of close relationships with members of your own sex, and with those of the opposite?

- Which relationships do you find easier, and why?
- Do you belong to an all-male or an all-female group? If so, what needs does this meet? Does belonging to this group enhance or hinder your other intimate relationships?
- Re-read the section on language and intimacy. Do any of Tannen's observations apply to your experience?

FOUR

HISTORY AND CULTURE

There is a history in all men's lives
                                    Shakespeare[1]

Our ability to experience intimacy is greatly affected by our culture and family of origin. These factors determine both our expectations of intimacy and also our ability to make close relationships. This chapter focuses primarily on influences that have affected Western culture, many of which tend to inhibit intimacy. Identifying and understanding these makes it easier to appreciate their effect on us, and even to make changes if we wish to do so. Many factors in present-day society which affect our ability to be intimate have their origin in history.

OUR WESTERN HISTORICAL HERITAGE

Greek Culture

Greek philosophy, particularly the ideas of Plato, strongly influenced Western thinking.[2] Plato contrasted the human soul and body. He taught that matter was evil, and as the body was matter it was inherently bad. He believed that the spirit or soul was essentially good, entombed in an evil body, waiting for death to experience its full potential. This led to a conflicting dualism.

To the ancient Greeks, our bodies differentiate us from one another, proving that we are separate. By contrast, the Hebrews believed that a human being did not *have* a soul but *was* a soul (*nephesh*). 'The LORD God formed man of the dust of the ground, and breathed into his nostrils . . . ; and man became a living soul.'[3] To them, the body is merely the outward manifestation of the person within. The fact that we each have a body is not something to separate us, but a common factor which unites us as human beings.

Separatist thinking predisposes to individualism, which is so prevalent in our culture today. It is true that each one of us is a unique individual, but accentuating individuality prejudices the development of community. This fundamental block has to be overcome if we are to be drawn towards intimacy.

The Renaissance

The word renaissance means 're-birth', and refers to the period in European history immediately following the Middle Ages. It started in the fifteenth century, with a surge of interest in classical learning and values and a revival of literature. The basic doctrine of Renaissance Humanism was: 'Human beings are the centre of the universe, limitless in their capacity for development.' This led to a drive to embrace all knowledge and fully develop our capacities. This belief is encapsulated in well-known statements by Renaissance architect Leon Alberti, such as: 'Man is the measure of all things', and 'A man can do all things if he will.'[4] Individual achievement was elevated to be the goal of life.

It is true that we all have enormous capacity for development physically, intellectually, emotionally and spiritually. Albert Einstein claimed that the average person uses less than ten per cent of their mental capacity. But an over-emphasis on self-development can lead to imbalance and a neglect of relationships with people and with God. Who we *are* is more important than what we do; *relationships* are more important than achievement.

Perhaps the most distinguished humanist was Rene Descartes, considered to be the father of modern philosophy.[5] He was a scholarly but solitary and introspective figure. He never married and biographers record that he did not attend the marriages of his brother or sister, nor was he present at the funeral of his father. Descartes believed in a mind-matter dualism, resembling Plato's spirit-matter dichotomy. He taught that the universe consists of two different substances: mind, or thinking substance, and matter which is basically quantitative. Only in humans are the two joined in substantial union.

He claimed that the human mind is reliable, and the only means of attaining truth. This gave rise to his famous aphorism, 'Cogito ergo sum' – 'I think, therefore I am.' Two legacies of the Renaissance, therefore, are an emphasis on intellectual ability and the supreme importance of individual achievement.

Industrialisation

The Industrial Revolution was largely confined to Britain from 1760–1830, but later spread to Europe, the United States and Japan. 'The industrial revolution is to be thought of as a movement, not a period of time.'[6] It was characterised not only by technical and industrial innovations, but significant social, political and cultural changes.

During that time, Britain changed from being an agrarian, handcraft economy, to one dominated by industry and machine manufacture. It was the start of the *urban drift*, as people looked for employment in the growing cities. In 1750, most of the population of England (and also the rest of the world) lived in rural villages. By 1850, fifty per cent of the population of Britain were living in towns and cities. The urban population drift brought with it horrendous social problems: poverty, overcrowding, sub-standard housing, 'sweated labour' (the exploitation of women and young children in the work force), hunger, prostitution, drunkenness, domestic violence and disease.

While many of these excesses and health issues were later corrected, urban population shift continues to this day, especially in developing countries. For the first time in history, more people throughout the world live in and around cities than in rural areas. By the year 2000, there will be over twenty megacities with populations of ten million or more. Tokyo, for example, will have nearly thirty million people.[7]

Apart from poverty, disease and other social consequences of human beings living together in vast numbers, the development of cities has a significant impact on family life and relationships. Cities foster competition which contributes to alienation and loneliness. Loss of the extended family, which was the way of life in rural areas, has had a big influence on people's experience of intimacy. Urban homes tend to contain two-generational 'nuclear' families, comprising one or two parents plus a small number of children. Usually they are cut off from the support of grandparents, aunts and uncles.

With the advent of factories, children and parents went out of their homes for work. Trades and crafts were no longer passed on within the family, with loss of this close interaction between parents and children. The locus of education moved from the home to the institution, with parents losing that vital role. Until the Industrial Revolution, education was of poor quality or non-existent for the working classes in England. Later, as educational standards improved and compulsory education was introduced, children tended to become better educated than their parents. This, too, widened the gap between the generations.

One significant feature of eighteenth-century Britain was the club. 'Men grew up in an environment of institutions which ranged from the cock-and-hen club of the tavern to the literary group of the coffee house; from the "box" of the village inn to the Stock Exchange . . . Every interest, tradition, or aspiration found expression in corporate form.'[8] While this may have been a natural reaction to the loss of other forms of intimacy, often these clubs were formed not so much for friendship as for business purposes or to provide pressure groups. Also, they were mostly clubs exclusive to men.

These three great historical influences: Greek philosophy, the Renaissance and Industrialisation have had a major influence on our attitudes and ability to experience intimacy today. But there are other more recent factors which affect us all.

MODERN CULTURAL INFLUENCES

Many twentieth-century advances have enhanced our way of life, particularly in the fields of health, education and environmental control. But certain aspects of our culture draw us away from community and the ability to experience intimacy. Some of these factors are the inevitable consequences of progress, and have to be accepted. We cannot put the clock back. The answer lies not in rejecting changes but in identifying them and bringing them into balance in our lives. Modern Western society can be described in various ways, and we will focus on some of the trends which militate against intimacy.

Technological Society

Since industrialisation started in the eighteenth century, our life-style has been more and more invaded and dominated by technology. With the advent of the electronic era in the 1950s and computer technology more recently, our lives are being increasingly controlled by machines and gadgets. These advances may reduce drudgery and make life easier, but at a price. In our materialistic society there is a temptation to love things and use people. Friendship and intimacy only become priorities when we love people and use things.

Consumer Society

As Western countries, in particular, move away from an agrarian to industrial lifestyle, more and more of the population are consumers rather than producers, takers not givers. In New Zealand, for example, 38.5 per cent of the male work force in 1896 were employed in agriculture, fishing or forestry. By 1996 this figure was down to 12.9 per cent.[9]

Before the Industrial Revolution, home was the site of reproduction and production. Now it is a place for reduced reproduction and the consumption of goods produced elsewhere. Consumerism and materialism are a way of life in the West. We are constantly bombarded on television, radio and through the mail by messages telling us that the way to happiness is in things. One cynic has described it in a parody of Descartes' famous words: 'I consume, therefore I am'!

There is nothing wrong with possessions. The question is do we possess them or do they possess us? Our goods and our toys need to be held on an open hand. A good metaphor is to see how much dry sand you can pick up in your hand. If you hold your hand flat and open, it will be a significant amount, though once your hand is full any extra will just slide off. But if you hold on to the sand with a clenched fist, most of it will be lost. So it is with our possessions. Only people with open hands have time for relationships. Henri Nouwen's prayer expresses it well: 'Please help me to gradually open up my hands and to discover that I am not what I own.'[10]

Instant Society

We are preoccupied with the quick gratification of our needs, from instant coffee and take-away meals, to instant relationships via dating services, or instant riches through lotteries. Anything taking time is suspect. Because time appears to be our most precious commodity, we spend money to save time. Time pressures dominate our lives, and we are often controlled by the clock. Working to 'deadlines' can erode relationships as well as health.

Many people equate busyness with success, which becomes the foundation of their identity and self-worth. Filling our lives with activity ensures that we have no time for reflection, let alone relationships. 'Such an attitude to life makes intimacy impossible because intimacy needs time.

It is very difficult to be intimate when you have to book friends or partners into the diary in order to be intimate with them.'[11]

Throwaway Society

Many consumer goods come in disposable containers and plastic bags. Some items are designed to be thrown away after use. Often it is cheaper and less time-consuming to purchase a new appliance than to have the old one repaired. In the city in which we live, each household generates over a tonne of disposable waste annually, and the amount increases every year.

But this 'Kleenex mentality' doesn't only apply to material things. Many moral values, standards and certainties that were taken for granted a generation ago have also been discarded. Along with them, people and relationships are often treated as dispensable. The attitude is: 'If a relationship ceases to be useful, I can do without it and find another.'

Mobile Society

On average, people move home in New Zealand every five years. On the West Coast of the United States it is estimated to be about every three years. People move for many reasons, such as work, education, boredom or as their economic status improves. As a result of frequent moves, extended families are split up, with consequent loss of closeness and support. Deep friendships are harder to maintain, and motivation to build intimate relationships is reduced if there is a likelihood of moving on in the near future. Travel is a popular pastime in New Zealand today. During the year ending March 1995, 23.2 per cent of the population were overseas for either business or pleasure.[12]

Individualism and Achievement

We have identified the roots of Western society's preoccupation with individualism and achievement in Greek philosophy and the Renaissance. These values are very much alive in the West, though they are not part of other cultures, such as in Asia or the Pacific Islands. Individual enterprise and achievement are commendable but are often associated with intense competition. This leads to alienation rather than community, loneliness rather than intimacy.

The writer of Ecclesiastes sums it up: 'I saw that all labour and all achievement spring from man's envy of his neighbour. This too is meaningless, a chasing after the wind.'[13] The danger inherent in achievement and individualism is selfishness, or at least a self-centredness. My needs and desires control my life. *Other-centredness* is essential for the development of deep friendships and intimacy. *Equality* is another value that is prized in Western democratic society, yet inequality between the sexes is still common. Equality is essential for meaningful human friendship and intimacy.

DOWNGRADING OF WOMEN

One significant factor which makes true intimacy difficult between the sexes is the way men have treated women down through the ages. Almost without exception in every culture of the world, men have treated women as inferior and subservient. The following are some comments on the Hebrew, Muslim and Christian traditions in respect to relationships between men and women.

Hebrew Tradition

Abraham, who lived about 2000 years BC, became the model for Jewish men. He was a Chaldean and brought with him well-defined attitudes to women. The records show that although Abraham and Sarah had a loving relationship, it was not an equal one. For example, when they moved to Egypt to escape a famine, he expected Sarah to lie by saying that she was his sister and not his wife, in order to protect him. He was even prepared for her to be taken into Pharaoh's harem – until God intervened. She was his property to do with what he liked, but not his equal.[14] Despite the shame, loss of face and dishonour to Jehovah that this action produced, Abraham repeated the trick twenty years later in a similar situation.[15] This provided a powerful model that his son Isaac followed.[16]

We obtain some insight into the relationship between husbands and wives in those days from Peter's writings: 'Sara obeyed Abraham, calling him lord.'[17] The actual word she used was *baal*. Husbands were treated as gods to be obeyed. Men could divorce their wives for any reason.[18] All they had to do was to clap their hands three times to dismiss a wife. Women were regarded as the property of their husbands. Moses was instructed to make a law requiring men to provide their divorced wives with at least a certificate of divorce.[19] Women could not divorce their husbands.

The Talmud is regarded as the most significant book in Jewish literature. It is a summary of the oral law that evolved over centuries of scholarly effort by Hebrew sages. Women were excluded from several important spheres of life, including the study of the Torah (the Law), 'which inevitably precluded them from playing a part in Jewish culture and spiritual life'.[20]

Talmudic sages on the whole did not regard women as inferior, but referred to them as 'a nation apart'. There are many stories in the Talmud showing that women were usually treated with respect. On the other hand, statements such as: 'There is no wisdom for a woman except at the distaff' reveal an ambivalent attitude.[21] This is reflected in the famous rabbinical prayer: 'Blessed art Thou, O Lord our God, King of the Universe, that Thou hast not made me a woman.'

Muslim Tradition

Nearly one billion people live in Islamic societies today, where frequently women are treated as inferior to men and often as virtual slaves, kept in strict 'purda'. The Qur'an states: 'Men have authority over women because Allah has made one superior to the other.'[22] A Muslim man can legally marry up to four wives at a time and cohabit with slave concubines. The Qur'an states: 'Marry what seems good to you of women, by two's, threes or fours . . . or what you right hand possesses.'[23]

'Temporary marriage' is a Shi'ite tradition, and can last from a few minutes to several years; a convenient arrangement for men away from home! A Muslim may divorce his wife at any time and for any reason. All he needs to say is, 'I divorce you' three times before witnesses and it becomes irrevocable.

A modern writer gives vivid insights into the outworking of this male chauvinism in a Muslim society:

> The authority of the Saudi male is unlimited: his wife and children survive only if he desires . . . From an early age a male is taught that women are of little value: they exist only for his comfort and convenience. The child witnesses the disdain shown for his mother and sisters by his father; this open contempt leads to scorn of all females. Taught only the role of master to slave, it is little wonder that by the time he is old enough to take a mate he considers her his chattel, not a partner.[24]

Christian Tradition

The Teachings of Jesus and Paul

The teaching of Jesus on marriage and the example of how he treated women paved the way for a change in attitudes, even if his hearers found it hard to accept.[25] He challenged the mores and gender values of his day, and provided the foundation for the emancipation of women. Jesus spoke to women with respect and was even willing to debate theological issues with them.[26]

He chose women as friends and companions. He treated prostitutes with respect and care.[27] He commended a woman's act of love and devotion as something which would always be remembered.[28] He showed great care for his mother even in his hour of death.[29] He entrusted a woman with the first news of the resurrection.[30]

Paul expanded on the teaching of Jesus, and first-century

Hebrew and Greek readers of his letter to the Ephesians must have been amazed to learn that Christian husbands had to actually love their wives!

> Husbands, love your wives, just as Christ loved the church and gave himself up for her . . . husbands ought to love their wives as their own bodies.[31]

Abraham and Sarah were their model for marriage. Sarah accepted the fact that if the crunch came, she would sacrifice herself for her husband. Paul is now teaching that husbands should be prepared to sacrifice themselves for their wives, as Christ did for the church. This was revolutionary, but a logical conclusion to the Christian definition of marriage: 'Submit to one another out of reverence for Christ.'[32] This principle establishes the equality of men and women, under the authority of Christ.

One observation we made during twenty-one years in Papua New Guinea was the effect of the gospel on the way men treated their wives. Throughout Melanesian societies, women are regarded as inferior to men. In the Sepik Province, where we lived, they were the burden bearers. At the end of a day a woman would carry home a heavy load of food, firewood and often a child as well, while the husband walked along empty-handed. Women were denied participation in religious practices, ate their meals separately from men and slept in different houses. A husband had the 'right' to beat his wife if she offended him.

When people became committed Christians, we noticed significant changes in their behaviour. Husbands were more caring of their wives and started sharing their loads. Centuries of negative attitudes are not reversed instantly, but one evidence of spiritual renewal in men was a change in their attitude to women.

Teachings of the Early Church
Despite the clear instruction of Jesus and Paul, the harsh misogyny of Judaism re-emerged in the teaching of many of

the Church Fathers. Augustine wrote in the fourth century, 'I do not see in what way it could be said that woman was made for a help for man if the work of childbearing be excluded.'[33]

Earlier, Tertullian had made a blistering attack on women: 'You are the devil's gateway; the unsealer of that forbidden tree; the first deserter of the divine law. You are she who persuaded him whom the devil was not valiant enough to attack. You destroyed so easily God's image, man.'[34]

Tertullian overlooked the fact that Eve was deceived before she disobeyed, whereas Adam deliberately chose to disobey! Women were considered inferior in mind and body to men; and men who really wanted to please God were instructed to have as little contact with them as possible.[35]

A significant misunderstanding is that for many centuries theologians taught that men were made in the image of God but that women were not, or at least only partly so. Tertullian's statement is an example of this, which Augustine endorses:

The woman together with her own husband is the image of God, so that the whole substance may be one image; but when she is referred to separately in the quality of help-meet, which regards the woman herself alone, then she is not the image of God; but as regards the man alone, he is the image of God.[36]

John Calvin said, 'Women are in the image of God in an inferior degree.'[37]

Luther did much to restore the dignity of marriage in a time when only celibate people were considered capable of true spirituality. However, he still taught that women's roles and status were limited:

Men have broad shoulders and narrow hips, and accordingly possess intelligence. Women have narrow shoulders and broad hips. Women ought to stay at home; the way they were created indicates this, for they have broad hips, a wide fundament to sit upon; keep house and raise children.[38]

This paternalistic limitation of women's roles totally ignores the command of God that both men and women together were to have dominion over the rest of creation.[39] 'God created men and women to be covenant partners – to image God together; to be co-stewards of creation's vast potential, and to share in the abundance of God's provision from the earth.'[40]

Many misrepresentations of biblical teaching have been handed down from generation to generation. Attitudes of male superiority, which were the norm in society, were 'baptised' by the Church.[41] In any relationship, if one party considers himself or herself superior to the other, deep intimacy is difficult or even impossible.

The Battle of the Sexes

The conflict between men and women goes back to the dawn of time. God's punishment for Eve's part in the rebellion was:

> I will greatly increase your pains in childbearing;
>   with pain you will give birth to children.
> Your desire will be for your husband,
>   and he will rule over you.[42]

The Hebrew word that is translated 'desire' is *teshugah*, and does not mean 'longing for' so much as a desire to control. The next use of the same word is when God says to Cain: 'Sin is crouching at your door; it *desires* to have you, but you must master it.'[43]

This word implies a power struggle with both trying to control the other. God predicted, 'he will rule over you', but *this was not God's plan*, because he had created man and woman equal. The future domination of women by men is the direct consequence of the fall. We have already referred to Abraham and Sarah as an example of how this domination was operating a few generations later.

Down through the centuries in every culture there is a

record of the battle of the sexes, with men claiming superiority to women. This is not only evident in Hebrew, Christian and Muslim traditions, but also in Western secular society. Sigmund Freud, the father of modern psychology, taught that women are defective males, 'doomed to unrelieved genital deficiency'!

This century has seen the rise of feminism, an attempt to bring balance back into the relationship between men and women. A major milestone was when women won the right to vote, first in New Zealand in 1893, later in the United Kingdom in 1918, in America in 1920 and as recently as 1973 in Switzerland. As women asserted their rights, this naturally led to a male backlash, which in turn has given rise to a radical response; what Germaine Greer calls 'revolutionary feminism'.[44]

But many secular and Christian writers present a balanced picture of women's perspectives in an attempt to establish their rightful place in what is still essentially a male-oriented world.[45] The issue of equal pay for equal work is still not resolved in many so-called democratic countries. On the whole, men still operate on the assumption that the male perspective on life is the norm and the female one is odd or defective. Bumper stickers proclaim: 'Women Can Do Anything', but they usually have to be twice as capable to receive recognition in a man's world!

Inequality between the sexes is an issue which all Christians should take seriously if they believe the words of Paul, that in Christ's Kingdom, 'There is neither Jew nor Greek, slave nor free, male nor female, for you are all one in Christ Jesus.'[46] The teaching and work of Jesus paved the way for us to deal with racial, social and sexual discrimination and injustice. The Church should be taking the lead in redressing these imbalances. Unfortunately, gender inequality is still present in the thinking of many Christians today. This is a serious block to the experience of true intimacy between men and women.

The factors that we have briefly explored will vary in the background of each of us, depending on our culture, sub-culture and family of origin. The attitudes and values of our immediate family as we were growing up are the most significant influences in our lives. All these factors and probably others are important, and we each need to consider how they may have influenced our ability to experience intimacy. While we are products of our past, we do not have to remain slaves to it.[47] We can change.

One consequence of the antagonism between men and women is that people frequently find it easier to relate to members of their own gender. This can result in rewarding same-sex relationships. But in some cases this has led to a genital expression of intimacy. Some people have moved into a homosexual or lesbian relationship, not because of sexual preference but because of their legitimate longing and need for intimacy.

INTIMACY AND ETHNIC CULTURES

So far we have looked primarily at modern Western society. It is interesting and instructive to compare and contrast attitudes to friendship and intimacy in the West with those of other cultures. Anthropologists have studied the phenomenon of friendship in various societies and have identified some striking differences. In a book of this nature it is only possible to give a few illustrations.

Many societies consider friendship to be as important as, or even more important than, marriage, and surround it with ritual and ceremony, including blood pacts. Herodotus mentions rites using blood among the Scythians, Medes and Persians, and they were widely practised in pre-Christian Europe. There have been many ethno-sociological studies in different cultures on these kinds of friendship bonds.[48]

Similar friendship pacts are made today, using saliva, beer or milk as well as blood. The symbolism of the Communion elements represent for Christians a deep friendship and bonding with Christ and with one another. Those who worship together often feel a closeness, though of itself this may not lead to intimacy.

In the early Middle Ages in Europe, blood pacts fulfilled the role of formalising and sacralising friendships.[49] The Church initially sanctioned this rite, but later the practice was banned and seems to have been replaced by godparenting. Adults often formed a close bond and friendship with the children of friends, for whom they became godparents.

Co-godparenting is a relationship between the parents and godparents of a child christened in church. It still exists in Europe and particularly in South America, where it is called *compadrazgo*.[50] This practice cements ties and strengthens relationships between friends and neighbours.

In Italy, the godparent is known as *compare*, a word also used for friend or colleague, and even for members of gangs such as the Mafia. The boss is known as the *padrino* or godfather. Gang members often display lasting loyalty to one another, albeit mostly through fear or because of family ties. The proverbial English phrase 'thick as thieves' indicates that kind of loyalty among people banded together for the purposes of crime.

In Australia, a cult of 'mateship' developed from the early days of European settlement and convict times. This bonding was strong among diggers, goldminers and bushrangers and varied from friendship to gang participation. These groups were almost exclusively male. Heroic self-sacrifice and loyalty often existed between mates, even though they seldom shared in the way we have defined friendship and intimacy. In Australia and New Zealand today, 'mate' is a loose term of friendship, but strangers can also be greeted with 'Hi, mate!'

A strong bonding often develops between soldiers who fought and suffered together. A common language provides a reason for friendship and loyalty when away from home. In Papua New Guinea, where there are more than 800 languages, people who speak the same language call each other 'wantok' (from 'one talk' or one language). Tragedy, such as a natural disaster often brings people and communities together. People who share a common illness, or who have relatives with similar conditions, may develop support groups and close friendships. Shared grief breaks down barriers.

Business friendships exist in many cultures, often expressed in trading relationships. These can cross hostile barriers between tribes. We lived in Port Moresby for six years, and sometimes attended the Hula Festival, commemorating the business friendship between the Motu people and tribes hundreds of miles away. The Motu sailed in their canoes to exchange pottery and ornaments for sago. They regarded their Papuan trading partners as 'best friends', with exchange of gifts, much embracing and protestations of love. Trade friendships exist in many other parts of the South Pacific and Africa.

Friendship is universal but has many faces. Our Western patterns of friendship are not the only ones. People vary in what they want from a friendship, and no one can presume on the expectations of another. Just as loneliness is related to discrepancy between the expected and achieved levels of social contact, so satisfaction from friendship or intimacy depends on the degree to which a person's expectations are met. These expectations are heavily influenced by our culture and upbringing.

Summary

Many factors in our heritage combine to affect our ability to make intimate relationships. While our personal modelling is the most significant influence, historical events over the centuries are also important because they have affected our culture and some have diminished our ability to be intimate. The down-grading of women, and gender conflict are serious handicaps to intimacy between the sexes. Understanding cultural perspectives helps us appreciate the complexity of intimacy in human relationships.

REFLECTIONS AND EXERCISES

1. CULTURAL INFLUENCES   Re-read the section headed Modern Cultural Influences, and reflect on the issues mentioned there which impact on your life. 'I consume, therefore I am' is a rather cynical description of prevailing attitudes, but it is salutary to reflect on the subtle influence of consumerism.

   Discuss the following simple tests in your group:

   • How many new gadgets have you acquired in your household during this past year?
   • To what degree are you self-sufficient in terms of what you eat or make?
   • Count the number of items that you are encouraged to purchase in one hour's viewing of television.

2. POSSESSIONS   Reflect in your journal on the degree to which you are able to hold your worldly possessions 'on an open hand'. To what extent do you own your possessions and how much do they own you?

   • Couples would find it useful to talk this over together.

3. Has your home ever been broken into? Apart from the distress caused by this invasion of your privacy, how disturbed were you by the loss of your property?

4. FRIENDSHIPS   How many times have you changed residence in your lifetime. What effect has this had on the number and quality of the friendships you have made?

5. How many good friends have you *not* contacted in the past six months?

   • What are the reasons for this?
   • Do your friends mainly contact you, or do you mostly take the initiative to contact them?

- What do your findings suggest about the importance of people in your life? Is there anything you would like to change?

6. GENDER ISSUES   Reflect in your journal on your attitude to people of the opposite gender. Be as honest as you can. It might help to discuss this with someone who knows you well, or in your group.

   - What are the main factors responsible for your attitude to women or men? Think about the influences of your home of origin, your peers, the teaching of your church or things you have read.
   - For marrieds: How do you apply Ephesians 5:21 in your relationship?

7. In your small group, discuss the amount of downgrading of, or prejudice against women that you are aware of in the circles in which you move.

   - Is there anything you can do to help correct this?

FIVE

INTIMACY WITH YOURSELF

Know Thyself
Socrates, 470–399 BC[1]
Examine yourselves . . . prove your own selves
St Paul, AD 10–67[2]

Having defined intimacy in the last chapter, we now look at ways we can prepare ourselves to experience intimacy. The first step is to have an intimate relationship with myself, and this starts with really knowing who I am. It is not possible to understand another person well until I know and understand myself. Discovering the unknown starts with the known.

KNOW YOURSELF

'*Know thyself*' summarises much of ancient Greek philosophy, and Paul's injunction to 'examine yourselves' is an essential part of growing in the Christian faith. He encourages us all to 'have a sane estimate of your capabilities'.[3] This means having a balanced and honest view of myself. If I do not know myself I will be unable to reveal who I am to you. If you do not know me and I do not know you, we have no basis for intimacy. This is also true in developing intimacy with God, which is explored in chapter ten.

There are many ways to discover who we are and to know ourselves better. We will focus here on three aspects of this process, starting with increasing *self-awareness*. This means finding out more about the unique person I am, understanding my strengths and weaknesses, how I react to life, to others and to God. Another important part of who we are is our *sexuality*. This is an aspect of life that many people have not thought much about, are uncomfortable with or may be afraid to explore. But it is not possible to know myself fully without understanding my sexual nature. A third way of knowing myself better is to explore my *personality*. There are a number of useful tools available to help us do this effectively.

SELF-AWARENESS

While the goal of intimacy is a close relationship with someone else, the process starts as I develop a healthy relationship with myself. It is surprising how many people have never given much time or thought to this. We ourselves had little self-awareness until we were in our early forties, partly because of being preoccupied with our careers and family life, but also because we had never been exposed to the need for self-understanding.

For me (John), my journey in self-awareness began with reading Paul Tournier's book, *The Meaning of Persons*.[4] I clearly remember the occasion when I started to read it, travelling in a small single-engined aeroplane, high above the rugged terrain of Papua New Guinea. The reflections of this Christian doctor on existential issues as well as everyday experiences, illustrated by stories of real people, made me painfully aware of my ignorance of myself. It gave me a hunger to read the works of people who had thought about and explored the meaning of life. I also developed a new perspective on the Scriptures and a fresh desire to read them. I found in the Bible a reliable source of information about human nature as well as about God's nature.

Growing in self-awareness has for me (Agnes), been like the slow opening of a flower from bud to blossom. I realise I will not reach full bloom here on earth, and there will always be unknown parts to discover. The stimulus for my growth in this area was shifting our focus from helping people physically through medical work to seeing each as a 'whole person', with emotional, intellectual, social and spiritual needs as well.

This encouraged me to challenge myself: was I growing towards wholeness in all these areas? John and I had a good working relationship as partners and parents. We loved each other deeply, but that was shallow compared with what we know of love now. Learning to share at a feeling level not only helped our intimacy to grow but also my self-awareness. We discovered a number of practical ways to enhance this growth.

Reading
A good place to start increasing self-awareness is by reading books on this theme. We find it helpful to read out loud to one another. This slows down the flow of information and allows both reader and listener to think through and discuss the ideas presented. We have read many books together over the past forty years, which has been a powerful intimacy-building activity in our relationship. It is wise to be selective in your reading because a wide range of books is available, some helpful and others misleading.

How can you be sure that everything you read is true? You can't! However, God has given us minds that need stimulation and challenge, and also his Holy Spirit to guide us into all truth.[5] *All truth is God's truth*, whether it has been revealed to a Christian or someone who is not. Truth is truth, and God is the 'fountain of truth'.[6] Submitting what we read to the plumb-line of the Word of God helps us sort out gold from dross.

A common tendency in people who discover new and exciting awarenesses in their reading is to inflict these pearls of wisdom on others. This does not make friends and influence people! It takes time to integrate new insights, to differentiate between the true and the false, the wheat and the chaff. An old proverb says: 'Practise what you preach.' A better maxim might be: 'Only preach what you practise.'

Sharing
But there is value in sharing our learning journey with others. While reading books stimulates us and enlarges our information base, it is important to have opportunities to discuss new insights about ourselves and life. Husband-wife interaction and family discussions provide ideal opportunities for this, where applicable. But we can all develop the friendship of someone with whom to share these things. An even better learning situation is to be *part of a group* set up to explore these issues and help each other grow. We describe this process in more detail later in this chapter.

Developing Objectivity
Absorbing new understandings about human personality, and having opportunities to share and apply them is a start to growing in self-awareness. Another important skill is the art of objectivity, seeing myself realistically. It is like sitting in a different chair and looking at myself from a distance. This process becomes easier with practice. Feedback from others will help me check the reality of my self-awarenesses. Counselling and psychotherapy is largely a process of assisting people to become more self-aware.

A parallel skill is the ability to see other people objectively, especially people with whom we are emotionally involved. This is called empathy. Sympathy is feeling *for* a person in their situation or pain. Empathy is feeling *with* a person. It means seeing the world from his or her perspective, while maintaining relative detachment. These twin aspects of seeing ourselves and others objectively are needed for the development of true intimacy.

From our experience in working with couples, it seems that women are usually better than men at both processes. But all of us need to develop these skills, as they do not come automatically. The ability to see ourselves objectively helps us to do the same for others. You can only give to others what you have yourself.

David asked God to help him in this process of self-awareness: 'Search me, O God, and know my heart; test me and know my anxious thoughts.' To the Hebrews, the heart referred to the innermost being, the core of the self.[7] David realised that God had already searched him and knew him, so clearly he was asking for help to become more self-aware.[8] This self-awareness applies to many areas, but one that is often poorly understood is sexuality.

SEXUALITY

The word sexuality comes from the Latin word *sexus*, meaning to divide – referring to our male and female differences. While our sexuality *divides* us into two groups, it is also something that *unites* us. The most profound statement about sexuality is found in Genesis:

> God created man in his own image,
>   in the image of God he created him;
>   male and female he created them.[9]

Our dignity, significance and worth as human beings rests on the fact that we are created in God's image. This refers to many things, such as our spiritual nature, our personhood, our ability to reason, be creative, relate, love, make choices, and much more. But it is interesting that this text does not mention any of these important things. The only way stated here in which we resemble God is in our sexuality. Women and men mirror something of God in their femaleness and maleness, and together reflect his image. Karl Barth taught that the relationship between male and female is the human expression of our relationship with God.

So it is important to understand and be comfortable with our sexuality, as there is confusion about this important aspect of who we are. Many people grew up in homes where the subject was seldom mentioned, and have been hurt in the development of their sexuality through ignorance. Others have been abused in this precious part of them.

One place where sexual healing and transformation should be available is in the Church. But often church is experienced as an environment of judgement, condemnation and fear, due mostly to ignorance and lack of teaching.[10] We believe that understanding and accepting our sexuality is essential for healthy growth and wholeness, and also for the ability to make intimate relationships. We will focus briefly on four aspects of our sexuality: biological sex, gender identity, sexual identity and animus/anima.

Biological Sex

At a physiological level, the sex of a person is the result of pure chance, depending on whether a sperm containing an 'X' or 'Y' chromosome reaches the ovum first. But from a faith perspective, it is God, the Designer of our genetic make-up, who determines our sex.[11] We have worked with people who struggle with having been 'born the wrong sex'. Their deep lack of self-worth sometimes comes from the fact that their parents did not accept them as they were, but had wanted a child of the opposite sex. To know that my sex is determined by God helps in building a secure identity.

Gender Identity

Our gender identity is determined by rearing and social factors. Boys and girls are usually dressed differently, starting with either blue or pink booties! They are expected to play with different toys and be interested in different games. Different expectations are put on girls and boys in terms of their interests and future occupations, by both parents and society.

These factors vary from culture to culture and family to family, but our core gender identity is established by about the age of three. Religious beliefs and biblical interpretations affect our attitudes and behaviour later as adults. Over the past decade or so these gender expectations have been challenged, particularly in the Western world, with consequent blurring of gender differences. There is a drive towards unisex in such things as dress, hairstyle and occupations. Our upbringing has a large bearing on how we view ourselves as men or women, and gender consciousness is an essential aspect of knowing who we are.

Understanding our gender identity is part of healthy self-awareness, especially if we can eliminate stereotypic prejudices. This applies to feelings. For example, some men have been brought up to reject expressions of tenderness as 'un-manly' and always to project a tough exterior, when this may not be true to their real nature. Many women have been taught that assertiveness or expressions of anger are inappropriate. We will return to these behaviours later, as they are important in relation to intimacy. A realisation that we all are made in the image of God helps us to accept parts of our nature which might be regarded as more appropriate for the opposite gender.

Sexual Identity

Our sexual identity is how we view ourselves as sexual beings. Healthy sexual identity is when a person who is biologically female fully identifies with being a woman, and vice versa for males. Sexual identity is closely related to gender identity, but is not the same. For example, some women with a somewhat masculine gender identity (sometimes referred to as 'mannish') actually have a strong feminine sexual identity. Whereas, it is known that women with a lesbian sexual orientation may have either a male ('butch') gender identity, or a more typical female gender identity. 'Gay' men can be either macho or effeminate.

The greatest influence on our sexual identity is our *parental modelling*. Parental attitudes towards sexuality start to be picked up by children before they can communicate verbally. A parent's attitudes towards him/herself, the other sex, the child and about sexuality are absorbed from an early age.

Many children grow up in homes where they receive little or no sex education, and their natural questions about sex are met with either embarrassed silence or a reprimand. A strong message that we both learned in our childhood was, 'Don't talk about sex!' One thing that helped us personally in the expression of our sexuality was when we were free to talk openly to one another about what we needed and what we did not want in our love-making.

One significant area where parental influence has been shown to be crucial is the development of *homosexuality*. Research has established that one to two per cent of the population have a homosexual identity.[12] A homosexual is someone who is biologically male or female but is attracted sexually to members of the same rather than the opposite sex. This confusion of sexual identity is very painful, and is made worse by prejudice and homophobia in society.

Dr Elizabeth Moberly, a Christian research psychologist from Britain, has put forward a valid theory about the development of sexual identity.[13] She has shown that the main factor determining a heterosexual or homosexual identity is whether a child has received or been denied same-sex parental love. By the same token, a significant influence in the healing of a homosexual identity is experiencing same-sex, non-erotic unconditional love. It is tragic that in the Church, which should be characterised by love, acceptance and healing, people with a homosexual orientation often experience misunderstanding and rejection.

Animus/Anima

Carl Jung taught that in the unconscious depth of men there is a female archetype, or primal aspect. He called this the *anima* (Latin for 'soul'). Similarly, in every woman there is a masculine aspect, or *animus*. All men have within them a softer, nurturing side, but this is often covered up by gender conditioning, e.g. 'Big boys don't cry'. Women have strengths, normally defined as male traits, which are often hidden or denied. Jung contended that part of the process of maturity involves coming to terms with our 'contrasexual' natures.

Discovering and being comfortable with our gender and sexual identity, as well as understanding something of our subconscious sexual nature, is essential for self-awareness. Probably all of us have been impaired to some degree in our sexual development and require healing.[14] Informed awareness of our sexuality is a good place for this healing and growth to start. Another way to discover more about ourselves and increase our self-awareness is through personality tests.

Personality Tests

A number of instruments for assessing personality are available. The earliest one was developed by the Greek physician and philosopher, Hippocrates, in the fifth century BC. He believed there were four 'humours' in the body which accounted for four temperaments: *Choleric* – active, practical, 'hot-tempered'; *Melancholic* – emotionally sensitive, analytical, gifted; *Phlegmatic* – cool, calm, easy-going, balanced; *Sanguine* – warm, lively, buoyant. This analysis is still used by some people, but has limitations.

A well-known test is the Minnesota Multiple Personality Inventory, which picks up personality disorders as well as personality traits. The California Psychological Inventory assesses normal adult personality and is used as an aid to educational, clinical and vocational guidance. Another good one is the Sixteen Personality Factor Questionnaire. The Enneagram identifies nine personality types, showing how behaviour in later life is influenced by decisions made in childhood. Various aptitude tests can evaluate people's work potential in industry.

Personality tests are not perfect, and must be used in conjunction with other information. But they can increase our self-awareness and objectivity and help us discover our strengths and gifts as well as identify weaknesses or growing areas. The following is a brief description of two tests with which we are familiar. They are useful in understanding ourselves, and assisting others discover their own uniqueness.

1. Myers Briggs Type Indicator (MBTI)

Isobel Myers and her mother Katharine Briggs devised the 'Type Indicator' to help people understand their personality.[15] Their theory was developed from the work of Carl Jung in the 1920s on personality.[16] The MBTI test identifies four basic *temperaments* and sixteen *personality types*. The analysis is based on a person's preferences in four pairs of opposites:

- *Extraversion (E) vs Introversion (I)*   Extroverts thrive on sociability and derive energy from people. Introverts 're-charge their batteries' within themselves.
- *Sensation (S) vs Intuition (N)*   This dimension assesses the way we gain information from the outside world, either using our five senses – what we see, hear, touch, taste and smell (S); or by relying more on our intuition (N).
- *Thinking (T) vs Feeling (F)*   This pair identifies whether we make decisions primarily on thinking and logic (T); or by relying mainly on human values (F).
- *Judging (1) vs Perceiving (P)*   This evaluates our preference for closure and tidy organisation (J); or else a flexible and open-ended view of life (P).

It is well known that different personalities react to situations in different ways, including response to loneliness and intimacy. There is no right or wrong way. Our personalities are a given from birth and we cannot change our basic personality or temperament. Rather, we need to understand ourselves *to fully become* who we were created to be.

The way to grow and mature as a person is to develop the non-preference (or 'shadow' aspects) of one's personality. Understanding my temperament, and also that of someone

I wish to be close to, leads to greater acceptance of one another and improved communication. This assists growth in intimacy. Discovering our personality type also helps us to find ways of praying that are more appropriate for us, enhancing spiritual growth.[17]

Deborah and Paul were attracted to each other from the day they met. She was outgoing and vivacious, and he communicated a quiet strength. Deborah appreciated Paul's ability to sum up situations and come to clear conclusions. Paul loved Deborah's warmth, perceptiveness and spontaneity. Opposite characteristics attract us initially, but in the closeness of marriage can become hard to live with.

Three years after this young couple married, they found their differences almost intolerable, so sought marriage counselling. Each blamed the other for deliberately sabotaging the relationship. Deborah saw Paul as cold and unfeeling – 'with ice in his veins' – unable to meet her emotional needs. Paul described Deborah as 'moody, unpredictable and illogical'. There were few days without a fight or some misunderstanding between them.

We asked them to do the MBTI test to identify their personality types. Deborah's profile was ENFP and Paul's ISTJ, so in each of their preferences they were opposites. We encouraged them to see that none of their traits were 'good' or 'bad'. They just reflected the way they were made and represented their own uniqueness and gifting.

Deborah, was a 'people person', sensitive to relationships but found confrontation difficult. She was full of new ideas and disliked routine. Paul was more organised, hard working, and traditional. As an introvert, he preferred to spend an evening at home listening to music or reading a book, whereas Deborah liked to socialise. He made decisions on facts and logic, but she came to conclusions as a result of 'gut feelings'. His meticulous tidiness was a pain to Deborah; her disorganised spontaneity drove him crazy!

Understanding their personality characteristics gave them

fresh insights about themselves and each other. Instead of seeing the other as deliberately difficult or provocative, they realised that each was being normal. This provided rational explanations for what was happening in their relationship, which especially appealed to Paul. They were not 'bad' or 'crazy' after all. They still had a lot of work to do to accept and appreciate each other. However, they now saw their differences as complementary rather than competitive. Once again, they began to love the differences that first attracted them to one another.

2. Taylor-Johnson Temperament Analysis (T-JTA)

The MBTI evaluates who we *are* and the T-JTA assesses who we are *becoming*. The Taylor-Johnson test[18] is designed to measure nine common personality traits:

> Nervous vs composed; depressive vs light-hearted; active-social vs quiet; expressive-responsive vs inhibited; sympathetic vs indifferent; subjective vs objective; dominant vs submissive; hostile vs tolerant; self-disciplined vs impulsive.

The results of the test are converted by means of tables into a percentile, which places a person within the context of a hundred 'normal' people in terms of each trait.[19] These particular traits were selected because they are important components of healthy living and interpersonal relationships.

Another advantage of this test is that the respondent can not only evaluate him/herself but also significant others, such as a partner. We find this useful for couples, providing them with some objectivity. It is an ideal tool for pre-marital, marital, and family counselling and is useful in other pastoral or counselling situations. Individuals discover through this test something of their relationship skills (or lack of them) and are made aware of areas where they could make changes. The nine personality traits correspond with the nine fruits of the Spirit.[20] Reflecting on this provides opportunity to relate spiritual growth to personality development.

Factors Influencing Relationships

Some of the essential things that we need to know about ourselves greatly affect our relationships. Figure 11, which we call the *iceberg model of relationships*, summarises a number of these factors. Many of them have been referred to already. Nine-tenths of an iceberg is below the waterline, and it is like this with relationships. What we see above the surface is only a fraction of the whole person. Most of who we are is below the surface in our subconscious. Deeper layers affect those nearer the surface, just as when the surface of the iceberg is altered or removed, more ice comes up from below. The four levels in the diagram are four aspects of ourselves which affect our ability to establish intimate relationships.

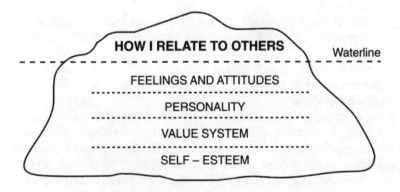

Figure 11. The Iceberg Model of Relationships

Feelings and Attitudes

Our initial response to people is often governed by our feelings, which in turn are mostly determined by thoughts and attitudes. For example, if I feel threatened by you I will keep away. If I don't like you I may react with anger and aggression. If I am feeling sorry for myself and preoccupied with problems I will probably ignore you, whereas if I am happy about life I am more likely to reach out to you.

Mature people are *in charge* of their feelings (without denying or repressing them) and do not allow feelings to control them. However, if I am not aware of my feelings and do not deal with them properly, they are likely to be out of control. In terms of intimacy, sharing feelings is the way to become close.

So, if I do not pay attention to my feelings, the prime ingredient of intimacy is lost. My feelings may still be apparent to another through my body language. The body does not lie, only the tongue can do that. In intimate relationships it is essential to be able to share real feelings without dumping them on one another. Sharing feelings is not easy. This process will be explored further in the next chapter.

Personality

Feelings are a normal healthy part of us, but they fluctuate along with circumstances. Our personality is much more constant, and is a combination of who we are plus who we are becoming. I cannot change my basic personality, but I can do something about my temperament and learn new behaviours.

For example, a thinking (T) person could develop more sensitivity in the feelings area (F); intuitive (N) people could become more aware of facts and detail (S). An anxious person can become more relaxed; an angry person learns to use anger appropriately. We can co-operate with God's Spirit in becoming the people we were designed to be. God does not change our personalities but refines them, so that we may become mature.[21]

Understanding my own and the other person's personality plays a big part in whether our relationship becomes a success or struggle. We all have areas where we have been damaged and need healing. Being unaware of this, or unwilling to do something about it, hinders the development of intimate relationships. For example, a needy and dependent person drains his partner's energy. An insecure person often tries to control others.

Value System

As we go through life we develop a value system, world view, or vision for life which determines much of our behaviour.[22] Our world view is our philosophical or spiritual basis for living, our reason for being. This determines our beliefs, priorities and motivation. In Hebrew thinking this is our 'heart', or centre of being.[23] The heart is the place where the personality can experience radical change, where we can be renewed in our spiritual nature.[24]

Self-Esteem

We have placed self-esteem at the bottom of the diagram, to emphasise that how we feel about ourselves affects everything else, especially relationships. Renewal of our value system will obviously affect our sense of self-worth. A change from a negative to positive self-image has a profound effect on our value system, personality, attitudes and feelings. This in turn improves our ability to relate with people and with God. It allows us to forget about ourselves and focus genuinely on others.

VALUE YOURSELF

Many people do not really value themselves and may not even like themselves. This is the background of numerous problems. A distorted view of one's self feeds a negative view of life. It is part of the cause of such conditions as depression, stress and burnout, and the breakdown of relationships in families and society. We have explored the consequences of low self-esteem in our book *Created for Love*.[25] We suggest there some practical ways to change this negative view of self and to grow in self-esteem. It is possible to develop a healthy sense of self-worth, to see yourself as God sees you and to value yourself. Here are five steps in this journey.

Know Yourself

The foundation of understanding who you are is knowing yourself. We are all in essence two people: the self of experience (the Person) and our self-picture (our Personage).[26] The former is the self of *reality* and the latter is the *role* that we often present to others. A healthy blending of the two enables people to become *real*.

Accept Yourself

Acceptance is powerful medicine. When you experience the acceptance of others, just as you are and without any requirement to prove your worth, you begin to feel worthwhile and lovable. To know the acceptance of others, and of God, helps you to accept yourself. This includes accepting your body, sexuality, personality, strengths, weaknesses, and your uniqueness. If you accept yourself you can more readily accept other people, which is an essential requirement for intimacy.

Love Yourself

This means to respect, honour, value, cherish, esteem and care for yourself. It is different from self-centredness, and people who love themselves in this sense have less temptation to pride and selfishness. In fact, they are able to forget about themselves and be other-centred. They are now free to love others unconditionally, as we cannot give to others what we do not first have ourselves. This is the concept behind the biblical command: 'Love your neighbour as you love yourself.'[27] Loving yourself is loving what God loves. Respect for yourself frees you to respect others, and mutual respect is the soil in which true intimacy grows.

Be Yourself

Once you know, accept and love yourself it is possible to be yourself without pride or false humility. You can relate to others authentically in all you say and do. Rather than *react* to others or the circumstances of life, you can *act* out of the integrity of knowing who you are. This leads to confidence and the ability to be assertive without being aggressive.

> Within you is written your own song –
> sing it with all your heart.

Share Yourself
People who are real find building an intimate relationship with another authentic person a natural process. They can lower their 'masks', or come out of their 'castles' to meet each other.[28] The process of self-revelation is a profound way of learning to know and accept ourselves. Conversely, the more we are comfortable with ourselves the easier it becomes to share ourselves with others. This is an application of the truth Jesus stated: 'Whoever has will be given more, and he will have an abundance.'[29]

DEVELOP YOURSELF

We have all been created with tremendous potential in every area of our lives, much of which is untapped in a person's lifetime. It has been estimated by those who have studied the mind that few people use more than about ten per cent of their brain ability. Many people go through life unaware of the power and freedom of being in touch with and using their emotions. The potential for spiritual growth is unlimited, or limited only by our lack of desire for it. There are a number of practical things we can do to assist personal growth and develop intimacy with ourselves.

Journalling

We both find that using a journal helps in developing self-awareness and emotional and spiritual growth. A journal is not the same as a diary of events, but is a record of life's *journey*.[30] It provides a way of exploring the meaning of life, reflecting on who we are and who we are becoming. Keeping a journal has helped me (John) to move more from my head to my heart and to co-ordinate my 'nut' and my 'gut'. Much of my journal (Agnes) is my journey in prayer as I express my inmost thoughts and desires, writing them down 'with God watching', asking him to 'search me and know my heart'.

We use our journals for a number of purposes:

- To reflect on significant personal events, and process feelings about them such as grief, joy, frustration, anger or confusion.
- To define and up-date our goals regularly, and provide some accountability for these.
- To record prayers. Doing this in dialogue form is sometimes helpful.
- To reflect on insights about ourselves, life or God.
- To record and process significant dreams.
- Keeping a record of 'pearls' from our reading of Scripture and other books, which provides a valuable resource.

These are just some ways a journal can be used as a tool for growth. It is a private document. We do not read each other's journal, though sometimes share bits we have written. Journalling is an effective way to develop yourself. Someone described keeping a journal as the most inexpensive form of psychotherapy! One practical book that has been a help to us is *Life Path: Personal and Spiritual Growth Through Journal Writing*, by Luci Shaw.[31]

Meditation

The meditation process is described in more detail in chapter ten, and is an important way of developing intimacy with God. We are not referring here to Eastern meditation, which is essentially emptying the mind. Christian meditation is a process of 'filling your mind and meditating on things true, noble, reputable, authentic, gracious – the best not the worst; the beautiful not the ugly; things to praise, not things to curse.'[32] In short, it is filling the mind with God himself. We find that by drawing aside in solitude to meditate, we also learn much about ourselves, as a by-product.

Dreams

Every person dreams for about an hour each night and adequate dream sleep is necessary for good health. Dreams are important in many cultures, but are usually neglected or dismissed as meaningless in our Western, secular world. This is because our rationalistic, materialistic values have their roots in the philosophy of Aristotle. He dismissed the validity of non-physical sources of knowledge, and taught that we receive knowledge *only* via the five senses or through reason.[33]

Rationalism infected the Church over the centuries and today many Christians are unaware of the value of dreams. This is strange, as one third of Scripture is related to dreams, visions and their interpretation. The Bible has over 200 direct references to dreams and visions. Dreams are personal, and almost all dreams have something to say about the dreamer. Other people in your dream usually represent an aspect of yourself.

Understanding dreams, especially vivid or recurrent ones, can tell us a lot about ourselves and increase self-awareness. Dreams are full of symbolism, and through this symbolic language we can get in touch with our sub-conscious selves (which comprises eighty to ninety per cent of who we are). God chooses to communicate with us all at times through our dreams, if we are prepared to listen. We have both had significant dreams which have helped us in times of stress and uncertainty. This is not the place to explore dream analysis further. Some good books that are available on the topic are listed in the references.[34]

These three growth skills are activities that people can develop on their own. But sometimes it is helpful to work through specific issues or problem areas with someone else such as a skilled counsellor, psychotherapist or spiritual director.

Counselling

Counselling is a process in which one person comes alongside another, helping him or her work through their problems and issues. A skilled counsellor does not do the work for clients. 'Give a man a fish and he will eat for a day; teach him how to fish and he will eat for a lifetime.'[35] In the same way, effective counselling is not solving problems but empowering people to grow and take responsibility for their lives.

Psychotherapy

Psychotherapy is a similar process, but usually deals with deeper issues buried in the subconscious, such as childhood hurts, identity problems and unexplored 'baggage' from the past. These hamper a person's development. The goal is the same as for counselling, to help people grow and to take responsibility for their lives, but the process may take a little longer.

Good counselling and psychotherapy have a wholistic perspective, embracing physical, emotional and spiritual issues. Requesting this kind of help is evidence of strength and a desire for wholeness, not weakness as some people think. It has been said, 'Everyone has a problem, is a problem or lives with one!' Psychotherapy can help people deal with blocks in their lives which prevent them from experiencing the intimacy they desire.

Spiritual Direction

This is a parallel process to counselling and psychotherapy, but in another dimension. The purpose is to assist another person in their prayer journey, helping him or her pay attention to God, who wants to communicate personally with each of us. The spiritual director encourages the directee 'to grow in intimacy with God, and to live out the consequences of the relationship'.[36] Having someone to look objectively at what is happening in my journey is the work of the spiritual director, who supports, reflects, clarifies and sometimes challenges me. This assists me become the person God wants me to be, continually growing and maturing in intimacy with him.

Growth Groups

A growth group is composed of a few people meeting together regularly to help each other grow in self-awareness and maturity.[37] Small group settings are powerful vehicles of healing. Howard Clinebell calls it 'People dynamic – the power we have to recreate each other and ourselves through sharing and caring.'[38] Growth groups function best initially with an experienced leader, whose main task is to ensure that it is a *safe place* for people to share and grow. As the group develops a life of its own, the leader can take less executive control. There are a number of essential guidelines for the proper functioning of small groups.

The ideal size is about six to eight people. In larger groups, some people may miss out on opportunities to participate fully. Regular attendance is important, as group dynamics alter when someone is missing. Some people find long-term commitment difficult, for a variety of reasons. A way round this problem is to meet for say six weeks and then re-negotiate for blocks of a few sessions at a time. This is better than allowing the group to disintegrate through attrition. One meeting a week is probably ideal. Allow one and a half to two hours per session. After about two hours the energy levels drops, especially with emotive topics. Starting and finishing times need to be defined and complied with.

The main task of the leader is to facilitate communication and interaction within the group. A good group is characterised by the following qualities. *Attentive listening.* When one member of the group is speaking, the others give the speaker focused attention. Comments by others should be directed towards clarification, not evaluation, *reflecting* back what they have heard. As we listen to others, so we learn to listen to ourselves, and to God.

It is important in a group to *speak for yourself*, allowing others to do the same. Offer to the group only as much of yourself as you feel comfortable in sharing, but be totally honest. Use 'I' rather than 'we' or 'you' statements. Sharing *feelings*, not just thoughts, develops self-awareness. Ideas separated from feelings become impersonal abstractions. Focus on the topic and *avoid distractions* or side issues.

For example, someone shared about the loneliness she experienced at boarding school. Another member of the group then started to give his views on the advantages and disadvantages of single-sex schools. While this was interesting, the original speaker felt devalued and hurt because the pain of her loneliness was not heard. The group is not the place for one person to analyse another's problem and practise amateur psychology. Let each person win his or her own battle, and do their own 'work'. The group is there to provide love and support in this task, not to give advice.

In every group some people talk more than others. It is important that everyone has a chance to participate and grow. Of course, everyone is also free *not* to contribute to a particular issue. Respect each other's autonomy and space. Do not be afraid of *silences*. Some people have an urge to rush in and fill gaps with talk. Shared silence provides a powerful opportunity for people to process what is happening for them. 'Speech is silver, silence is golden.'

Confidentiality is essential. Nothing destroys group trust more quickly than members talking with others outside about what has been shared in confidence. If members share a common faith, *prayer* with and for one another will unite and strengthen the group. But beware of using prayer as a 'quick fix', or a way of avoiding pain. Rushing to pray for people may prevent them doing the work they need to do.

There are many other kinds of small groups (see p 52) and these principles apply to most of them. Small-group experience exposes people to the dynamics of intimacy and can help them to risk intimacy in other relationships. Paul's metaphor of the body clearly teaches that we all need each other.[39] Body-Life is powerfully demonstrated by a small group that functions well.

Summary

Intimacy with another person is only possible if I have discovered a true intimacy with myself. This does not happen automatically, but comes when I learn to know myself. 'The longest journey is the journey inwards', and this is a life-long process. Some ways of self-development are learned best on one's own, but others require the help of another person, or a group setting. This book is designed to be used in all three situations.

REFLECTIONS AND EXERCISES

1. KNOWING YOURSELF   When did you last hear from yourself? Write a letter to yourself, describing what has been going on for you in the past week, month or year. Describe your feelings, hopes, fears, successes, failures, growing areas. Take your time and let it flow. You will learn a lot.

2. Write a description of yourself in your journal. What kind of a person are you? What are your values, goals, feelings about life? How do you think others see you? How do you relate to other people? Take time to fill out a true picture through which another person would really know you.

   • When you have finished, read it to a close friend, or your group, to obtain feedback on the accuracy of your self-picture.

3. SEXUALITY   Reflect on the following questions and write answers in your journal.

   • Recall your *earliest* memory related to sexuality: perhaps something someone said to you or did, or a question you asked. How old were you at the time? Do you think this experience had a positive or negative influence on your developing sexual awareness?
   • What specific *sex education* did you receive as a child and from whom? Were sexual matters talked about comfortably in your home? Were sexual organs referred to by their proper names? If not, what were they called? Did you gain the impression that sex was something good and beautiful, or bad and dirty?
   • What *attitudes* do you think you picked up from your parents about the opposite sex? Did you feel affirmed by both your father and mother in your own sexuality

as a girl or a boy? When did you start to feel good about yourself as a male or female?

- Talk about these memories in your small group, if you feel comfortable to do so. If you are married, share them with your partner.

4. VALUING YOURSELF   Make a list in your journal of ten or more positive adjectives that describe you, such as: hard working, honest, caring, confident, loving, thoughtful, creative, practical . . .

- Ask a friend to write a similar list about you and then compare them. What did you learn from this exercise?
- If you are in a small group, read your list to the others. When you have finished, the group can affirm you for the qualities that each one especially appreciates in you. Ask each person to add at least one more quality to your list. Take turns to do this.

5. JOURNALLING   If you have not done so already, start a journal. Choose a durable notebook, yet flexible enough to write comfortably. Date each entry. As an initial exercise, try the following.[40]

Find a comfortable place where you will not be disturbed, and relax for a while. Reflect on the idea of keeping a journal. When you are ready, write down what appeals to you about the process. What are the advantages and disadvantages? Does it make you feel vulnerable? Are you concerned about what you may find out about yourself? Does it seem that your thoughts and ideas are too trivial to write about? Are you afraid that someone might read it? Be totally honest and express your feelings as well as your thoughts. Enjoy what you are doing. Your journal can become an intimate friend and companion.

6. UNDERSTANDING YOUR DREAMS[41] Keep a small notepad, pencil and torch beside your bed, so that you can write down your dream as soon as you wake up, otherwise it will be lost. Remember Nebuchadnezzar's problem! (See Daniel 2.) Write down all the details, no matter how insignificant they may seem at the time.

The dream speaks symbolically. For example, what does a house in your dream remind you of, perhaps your childhood home? What experiences or feelings are associated with that house? What is happening in the structuring of your inner house? Are you adding on a new part to your 'house' or life. Each symbol has many possible meanings, and the real meaning can only be discovered by the dreamer. List all the associations until one seems to fit.

When a possible interpretation comes, test it in four ways:

a) Ask God for wisdom and insight.
b) Check it with Scripture. (God will not say one thing in the Bible and something contradictory in your dream.)
c) Talk it over with friends or someone experienced in dream work.
d) Pay attention to the feelings the dream left you with.

Understanding dreams takes practice. Read what you can about the subject, and don't be in a hurry to interpret someone else's dreams. Daniels are rare!

7. GROWTH GROUPS If you do not belong to a small group, why not consider starting one? Get together with some like-minded people and discuss the possibility. Use the guidelines listed in this chapter. Choose a topic or purpose for the group that appeals to all members. Working through a book like this one or our previous book, *Created for Love*, would give some structure and material to use.

SIX

BLOCKS TO INTIMACY

By wisdom a house is built, and through understanding it is established; through knowledge its rooms are filled with rare and beautiful treasures.

Solomon, c. 1000 BC[1]

Intimacy is a rare and beautiful treasure. It does not come into our lives automatically, but has to be desired and worked for. There are basic principles that help us build intimacy into our 'house'. There are also 'road blocks' within us, or 'baggage' we carry, which need to be cleared away before the building can start. This chapter looks at blocks to the development of intimacy, and the next chapter identifies important keys to achieving this goal. Some of these blocks have been referred to in previous chapters. Many people are not ready for intimacy, and moving into a close relationship such as marriage before having dealt with these issues will often compound the problem rather than ease it.

A common expectation is that a close relationship will make up for personal inadequacies. This is not true. In fact, closeness with another person *exposes* individual deficiencies. On the other hand, an intimate relationship also provides a situation where two people can help each other to grow, but each one has to do his or her own work. Unless this is appreciated, relationships can become very complicated and even destructive.

Neville and Jenny were attracted to each other in their first year at university and soon became good friends.

Neville was confident and outgoing. Nothing seemed to faze him and he always made problems look simple. He was good to be around, especially when Jenny felt depressed. She was insecure and unassertive. Although attractive and intelligent, she felt inadequate and saw most things in life as problems rather than challenges.

However, Neville appreciated the warmth of her loving nature and enjoyed helping Jenny with her difficulties. It seemed as if they had been made for each other, and fitted like a lock and key. They married after graduating, but three years later came for counselling. What had seemed an ideal relationship turned into a frustrating one. They still loved one another but could not understand why they also annoyed each other so much.

Eventually, they were helped to take the focus off each other's failings and look at their own 'baggage'. Neville realised that he derived a lot of satisfaction from solving other people's problems, and this was one of the things that had attracted him to Jenny. Certainly, she had many problems. He had become a live-in 'rescuer', and this was the main way he showed his love for Jenny. But he had needs too, which he often ignored, and he was unaware of his compulsive problem-solving behaviour.

On the other hand, Jenny was a competent person and despised herself for being so needy. She realised that she was dependent on Neville, partly to ensure that he gave her constant attention. The more she was rescued, the more dependent she became, which disempowered her rather than helped her. But they were willing to do something about their 'blocks'.

Jenny decided that she did not want to be rescued any more. While still welcoming Neville's encouragement, she began to take charge of her life. Neville realised that he did not need his 'rescuer mask' in order to be loved and started relating to Jenny as an equal. They had a lot of work to do, but when they stopped the 'psychological game' they were playing, they discovered more satisfying depths to their relationship.[2]

BLOCKS TO INTIMACY

There are a number of blocks on the pathway to intimacy, which are summarised in Figure 12. They are all inter-related, and so tend to be compounded. On the other hand, when one block is removed it has a positive effect and makes it easier to work on others.

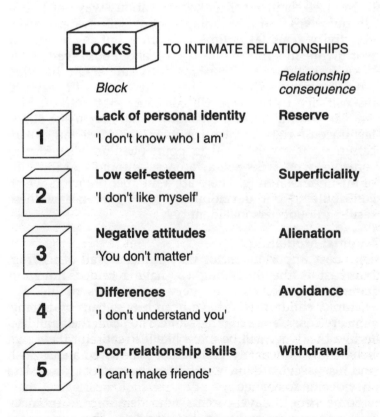

Figure 12. Major blocks to intimacy

These five blocks are aspects of *emotional immaturity*. The major task of growing up is developing maturity, without which we cannot have healthy adult relationships, let alone intimacy. We will now expand on these five major blocks and show how they can prevent the full experience of intimacy in a relationship. The diagram indicates the main consequences of these intimacy-limiting blocks: reserve, superficial behaviour, alienation, avoidance and withdrawal.

1. Lack of Personal Identity

In the last chapter we looked at various ways of knowing ourselves and developing healthy self-awareness and objectivity. This takes time and effort but is abundantly worthwhile in terms of how we feel about ourselves. It also helps in building relationships with others. On the other hand, inability to see ourselves objectively will result in insensitivity to the way we come across to others. This leads to communication breakdown and may make others feel uncomfortable, which results in avoidance rather than closeness. It can be hard to point out this behaviour to someone who lacks self-awareness without causing hurt or misunderstanding. There are a number of factors which contribute to our development, and ignorance of these results in poor personal identity.

Parental Modelling

The most important factor that influences all of us from our past is the modelling we have received from our parents, especially in the very early years of life. For example, children who have been brought up by parents who are considerate of others and who teach their children to live this way, will be more likely to monitor their own behaviour. Conversely, children of parents who are selfish and insensitive are likely to follow this pattern too, unless they decide to change.

Some people have parents who demonstrate intimacy with one another and with their children. They experience healthy expressions of intimacy through touch and sharing of feelings. But others grow up in homes where feelings are either dumped on others or else repressed, and where there are few expressions of affection. It is helpful to look back at your modelling and identify the influences to which you were exposed. This is *not* a blaming process but an exercise in awareness. You will probably discover some negative attitudes that have affected you. That is normal. Parents are not perfect, and we live in an imperfect world. These factors may have been *reasons* why you behave in a certain way now, but they are *not excuses*.

Discovering reasons for my behaviour helps me understand myself better, but using them as excuses to avoid making changes is self-defeating. The home provides our primary model, but many other influences affect us as we grow older. See Figure 13. Exploring our childhood background is a helpful process. Exercise 1 at the end of this chapter is one way of doing this.

Childhood Hurts and Fears
Past traumas profoundly affect the way we relate to others. People who have been abused emotionally, physically or

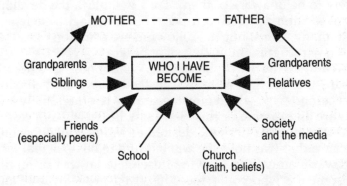

Figure 13. Our modelling

sexually, or who have experienced painful rejection, can move into life severely damaged. They may carry around buried grief, fear, anger, bitterness, or perhaps resentment towards authority figures or people of the opposite sex. But if they are unaware of how it has affected them, they will not realise how it influences their relationships. Also, they may not be aware of their need for healing of these deep hurts.

Fears often originate in childhood. If these are not faced and dealt with they can cripple a person in later life. People fear many things, such as failure, being controlled or hurt by others, or even being close to another person. Fear is a great enemy of intimacy. When Jesus was arrested in the garden, his best friends were so afraid that they deserted him and ran away.[3] 'Fear makes us move away from each other to a "safe" distance, or move towards each other in a "safe" closeness, but fear does not create the space where true intimacy can exist.'[4]

Defensiveness

In dealing with painful issues, we all use what psychologists call *defence mechanisms*. These are defined as: 'Ways people react to frustration and conflict by deceiving themselves about their real desires and goals in order to maintain self-esteem and avoid anxiety.'[5] They are subconscious processes, and a person with inadequate self-understanding is likely to be unaware of them. They will block the development of intimacy between people. Psychological defences take many forms, but the following are common ones that we may recognise in ourselves or others.[6]

Denial This is probably the commonest defence. It means the inability or refusal to see that we are behaving in a certain way, which may be obvious to others. Sally and Bill are an example of this. Sally saw her fiancé as a caring and attentive partner who desired an intimate relationship, because that was how she wanted him to be. In actual fact, Bill was mainly interested in himself. He saw her primarily as someone who could meet his deep need for love and affirmation, something which he had missed in childhood.

This realisation did not register with Sally until they had been married for a number of years. By then she was drained of emotional energy from having given so much and received so little in return. Bill was also in denial about his own behaviour. Denial enables us to overlook things that are too painful, pretending they do not exist.

Rationalisation This means a justification of unacceptable attitudes or behaviour, and often accompanies denial. It is a process of building up excuses to explain away behaviour. Initially, Sally justified Bill's selfishness in terms of, 'He's so tired after a busy day at work', or 'I musn't complain, he's a good provider and I know he loves me'. She justified her own responses by reasoning: 'This is the way a Christian should love, unconditionally . . . anyway, I should be submissive.' Eventually, she came to see that her own family model had prepared her to believe that this kind of behaviour was normal, because her mother and father related similarly.

Projection This means ascribing our own feelings or motives to others. Bill would accuse Sally of selfishness, if she went out for coffee with a friend, or if the meal was not ready when he came home. By the time they sought counselling help, they were accusing each other bitterly and were into the 'blame game'. They each projected their feelings onto the other, accusing one another of being angry and starting a fight. Projection is seeing 'the speck of sawdust in your brother's eye and paying no attention to the plank in your own eye'.[7]

Repression Unacceptable ideas, desires and impulses which are present in our subconscious are banished from our conscious awareness. The more Sally felt neglected and ignored by Bill the more she repressed these thoughts. Bill eventually became aware of his selfishness when it was pointed out, and realised that he had refused to own this behaviour over the years because it did not fit his concept of himself. Repression is the primary defence mechanism on which most of the others are based.

Bill and Sally really wanted a good relationship. When they took their eyes off each other's faults and focussed on their own behaviour and motives, they began to identify their own defences and saw how these had prevented intimacy. We all use psychological defence mechanisms, and as our self-awareness grows we become more sensitive to them. These defences are our 'blind spots' and most of us need the help of others to gently reveal them to us. But dealing with them needs more than awareness. It requires a change of 'heart', altering our value system (the core of the 'iceberg', see Figure 11, p 97) which affects the rest of life and relationships.

Life-Style Factors

We are all greatly influenced by the pressures of modern living and a society which communicates loudly that things matter more than people. If we are drawn into the philosophy that material possessions and financial security is what life is all about, we will not have much energy for spending time on developing our self-identity or intimate relationships.

2. Low Self-Esteem

People who do not value themselves or feel good about who they are, will be unlikely to want to know themselves better. Low self-esteem often leads to a fear of intimacy. If I do not like myself, I will be reluctant to reveal myself to you in case you do not like me either and reject me. Another possible consequence of making myself vulnerable and revealing myself is that people might take advantage of me or have some power over me.

So it is safer to stay inside my 'castle' and become a loner. How we feel about ourselves profoundly affects all our relationships. On the other hand, people who have a good sense of self-worth can forget about themselves. Healthy self-esteem frees us from an egocentric prison, enabling us to reach out to others in a natural way.

Masks

We have all learned to wear protective masks to cover up deficiencies, and show to others aspects of ourselves we think they will like. People with a low self-esteem wear masks most of the time, because they believe that others would reject them if they knew what they were really like. Masks provide protection, but they always limit intimacy. They are sometimes useful in impersonal or hostile situations, but totally inappropriate in the close-ness of an intimate relationship. Here are some typical masks. You may recognise them in others, or even in yourself.

Strong, silent type	Helpless dependent
Efficient problem-solver	Competent provider
Exuberant optimist	Moaning martyr
Party clown	The dunce
Negative cynic	Wise guy
Cool dude	Super-mum

There are many other masks that people wear. For some, they become 'personages' that are worn all the time, not just for occasional protection.

3. Negative Attitudes

The positive attitudes described in chapter two that are needed for friendship, such as love, acceptance, sincerity and other-centredness are required even more for the development of intimacy. When these are missing or replaced by negative attitudes, true intimacy is not possible. Negative attitudes towards people arise out of our basic self-centredness and selfishness. This results in the belief, whether expressed overtly or not, that my needs are more important than yours. Selfishness destroys intimacy quicker than anything else.

Selfishness is the natural outcome of unregenerate human nature. It is true that people display degrees of selfishness

and some may be less selfish than others, but we all naturally put ourselves first before others. Solomon described
this in terms of relationships: 'People who do not get along
with others are interested only in themselves.'[8]

Our basic attitudes are not going to change unless there is
a change within. Returning to the iceberg metaphor (Figure
11), we can alter the shape of the exposed part of the iceberg
and remove much of the surface, but it will be replaced by
more ice from below. But change in our 'heart' or value
system, which Jesus Christ can bring about, will renew
our attitudes from within. There are also a number of
distorted beliefs about intimacy that must be challenged
and changed.

Distorted Thinking about Intimacy

Our thinking determines our attitudes to life. Our minds
are shaped by past experiences, other people, our reading,
or teaching that we have received. Thinking can either be
distorted or valid, but it is not fixed. Distorted thinking
can be changed. We have suggested in *Created for Love*
an effective way of changing 'distorted messages' about
ourselves that we all carry around inside our heads.[9]

We are responsible to examine and challenge our beliefs,
discard those 'tapes' which are invalid and replace them
with new ones that are consistent with truth. Here are
four common distorted messages that people have about
relationships, which are all counter-productive to the development of true intimacy.

Belief 1 '*If I control the other person, we will stay close.*'

Insecure people often apply this belief to their relationships. There are many direct and indirect ways people use
to try and control others. These include making others'
decisions for them; manipulating them emotionally so that
they will stay close or dependent; threatening them in some
way, such as by withholding love, money or sex. Other
neurotic attempts to hold on to people include: inducing
guilt through acting as a 'martyr', developing an 'illness',

or using such statements as: 'If you love me you'll do as I ask.' Many children experience manipulation of this kind.

Controlling others has the *opposite effect* to developing intimacy; the other person will draw away or put up defences. This distorted message needs to be changed for a true one, such as: 'If you are free to be in charge of your own life, then we could be close.' Intimacy flourishes best between two people who control themselves, not each other. Love is caring enough not to hold on too tightly.

Belief 2   *'If I tolerate his/her selfishness he/she will love me.'*

Pretending something does not exist or does not matter is not the same as acceptance. It may seem to be a loving thing to do, but tolerating selfish or inconsiderate behaviour in people I love is really saying, 'I don't care about you, because I don't care that you are hurting yourself or others'. This is another example of denial. Real love cares enough to confront self-destructive behaviour that I may see in someone close to me. This is called 'tough love', and is an important part of intimate relationships.[10]

To ignore selfishness, self-destructive or relationship-destructive behaviour in someone I love is really encouraging it. It makes me a *co-dependent*. This has been defined simply as: 'When he has a problem and she helps him keep it. Co-dependency is her problem'[11] The gender roles may be reversed, but it is often this way round because men usually have a greater willingness to be cared for and women often collude with this. A co-dependent lets another person's behaviour affect him/her negatively and supports that behaviour.

For example, if I am close to someone who abuses alcohol or drugs, and I tolerate this or pretend it is not happening, I am actually encouraging the addiction. If someone I want to be close to is constantly withdrawing, hiding feelings, or using me in some way and I do not say anything about it, then I am encouraging the behaviour to continue. It is really saying, 'I don't matter, you don't matter and our relationship doesn't matter either'.

Respect is a foundation stone of intimacy, especially in marriage.[12] Being a co-dependent or becoming a 'door-mat' does not encourage respect from the other person. Tolerating insensitivity in another will not engender respect for that person either. It will lead to a cold relationship or to bitterness. The old distorted message must be changed to a conviction that: 'Intimacy grows in a climate of mutual respect, not tolerance.' Another variant of co-dependency is *relationship addiction*. This is any compulsive, possessive, manipulative relationship, and is false intimacy.[13]

False intimacy can take many forms, and has been defined as 'a self-created illusion to help a person avoid the pain of real intimacy'.[14] It is often manifested in one of the many forms of *sexual addiction*, such as an obsession with por-nography, promiscuity or obsessive masturbation. These are ways of seeking intimacy without a real relationship, with its potential for hurt and struggle. Another example is in a marriage, where a husband places excessive demands on his wife for sex, without consideration of her needs and feelings. This reflects both his emotional immaturity and her co-dependence.

Belief 3 'Conflict will inevitably destroy intimacy.'

Conflict in a close relationship is painful and a threat to intimacy as long as the conflict is unresolved. Trying to maintain 'peace-at-any-price' appears to avoid the problem, but actually increases the distance between two friends. Accumulated, unresolved conflicts build a wall between people, making them feel lonely and isolated. Burying something before it is dead does not get rid of it!

The fear of dealing with conflict is often based on the mistaken belief that anger is wrong. Anger is a healthy emotion that we are all born with, because we have been created in the image of God. God is love, but he is also angry at times. In fact, there are five times as many references in Scripture to God's anger as there are to man's anger. Anger is part of our 'survival kit', and a proper expression of anger is healthy. Repression of anger contributes to the build-up of many illnesses, such as depression. This was true for Jenny in the story earlier, and her depression lifted once she learned how to deal with her anger rather than repress it.

In our own relationship, we had a problem with anger. I (John) never saw my father angry. Conflict between my parents must have been resolved behind closed doors, 'never in front of the children'. I assumed from their example that good marriages never had conflict. This might seem a good model, and it was nice to live in a home without fighting or bickering. But I started life with a handicap. I had never seen two adults deal with their anger appropriately or work through some of their conflicts. So I assumed that conflict and anger would never rear their ugly heads in our marriage, and if they did it would be total disaster! When anger surfaced between us, I could not even acknowledge it, let alone deal with it.

I (Agnes) was brought up with a similar fear of anger. My father found it hard to confront anger, and seldom expressed his feelings. My mother was more expressive, but I did not see a practical model for dealing with anger either. Thus, we both brought to our relationship an inability to handle anger. We assumed that conflict would destroy intimacy and so we avoided it at all costs.

But as we grew in self-awareness and in the ability to express feelings to one another, so we discovered that anger need not be destructive. We are learning to take responsibility for our anger, express it to one another in healthy ways, and use conflict to build rather than destroy our relationship. We adopted the motto: 'Never waste a good conflict!' Working through conflict teaches us so much about ourselves and each other. Rather than destroy closeness, conflict can be used to build intimacy.

Belief 4 '*I expect my partner/friend to meet all my intimacy needs.*'

Many people believe this myth about relationships, whether in a close friendship or in marriage. 'This wonderful person will meet all my needs. He/she will know how I feel and will be able to take my unpleasant feelings away. I will never feel lonely again.' This is a beautiful dream, but not reality. The other person will never know how I feel unless I tell her/him. My feelings are mine and I am responsible for them. In an intimate relationship these feelings can be shared, which often brings healing. But my partner is not responsible for 'fixing' my feelings or taking them away.

There are many other needs that my partner cannot possibly meet. Nobody can give me maturity, I need to do the growing myself. Nobody can give me a sense of self-worth, I must take responsibility for my own self-esteem. Nobody can satisfy my existential loneliness, that is my personal journey. No person can give me spiritual life, because this results from a relationship with God. My partner can *help me* and encourage me in all of these areas, but cannot meet these needs.

No one person can meet all your intellectual, professional or social needs. You may have needs for friendship with people of a different gender from him/her. The unrealistic expectation that one person can meet all your needs can lead to the controlling, possessive scenario described above.

This distorted belief must be replaced with truth that intimacy grows when two people take responsibility for themselves. Maturity is a journey from *dependence* to *independence* to *inter-dependence*. As two independent people learn to become inter-dependent they discover the joy of intimacy. Healthy relationships require a balance between intimacy and autonomy.

4. Differences

Everyone is unique and different. Some differences are gender based, and others are more related to personality, as was discussed in the last chapter. Cultural differences vary widely, but even within cultures each person is influenced by the model their parents provided. As we grow up we develop different interests, tastes, likes and dislikes, ranging from food to clothes, hobbies, professions, music and sport. We differ in the way we use language, how we express love and caring for others, and the way we face life.

We are usually drawn to people who differ from us. At a distance, these differences seem interesting and attractive. But in the closeness of an intimate relationship, the very differences that appealed to us may become a threat. Sometimes an organised person is attracted to someone who is casual and spontaneous. A thoughtful and logical person is often attracted to a warm, sensitive, feeling person. This is fine until they try to make decisions together and they may end up accusing each other of being either cold and calculating or illogical and emotional! As we appreciate each other's differences we can combine them to enhance our relationship.

Terry, a quiet and rather reserved man was attracted to out-going and vivacious Kim. He finds conversation difficult at social gatherings but she thrives in this situation and talks to everyone. Terry admired the ease with which Kim coped so well in social situations, and she saw his quiet manner as a strength. But after they had been together for a number of years, he found her social skills a threat and she saw him as a bore. One day, Terry was talking to Bill at a party. Bill was also reserved, and his wife was a good socialiser like Kim. As they watched their partners interacting with guests, Terry said:

'How do you cope with your wife being so out-going?'

'I love it', said Bill, 'I never cease to admire her skills. I'm rather a slow learner, but she is teaching me to be a better communicator.'

Terry and Bill were both attracted to the same quality in their partners. For Terry it became a threat, but to Bill it remained a source of pleasure and encouragement.

Differences are a potential source of conflict in a close relationship and can block intimacy. Differences in others also force me to *assess myself*. If I am not really comfortable with myself, differences are more likely to threaten me. If I feel good about who I am, our differences can add spice to our relationship and provide opportunities to grow personally. The bigger the difference, the greater is the chance of conflict, but the potential for enriching an intimate relationship also increases.

5. Poor Relationship Skills

Healthy relationships and real intimacy depend largely on the quality of communication between the two people. However much friends care for each other, it will not be possible for them to be intimate if they cannot share the reality of themselves. We are not born with this skill, and few people are fortunate enough either to see good communication modelled for them in their family of origin or are taught it at school. Thus, most adults move into close relationships without the essential skills necessary to develop the quality of intimacy they may desire.

In chapter two, basic communication skills for developing friendship were described, and chapter seven focuses on specific skills needed to develop intimacy. While the principles are universal, communication between any two people is unique because they are unique individuals. Therefore if they are to develop intimacy, they must know each other well and learn to get through to one another in a way that is specific for that individual alone. Because each one of us is changing all the time, an intimate relationship between two people must adapt, grow and change too. This makes the journey of intimacy exciting and challenging.

Summary

Before two people can experience intimacy they must clear away road blocks or 'baggage' that prevent closeness. This starts with honest self-awareness, looking at our past experiences, present behaviours and defence mechanisms. Attitudes and beliefs must be evaluated to see if they are consistent with developing closeness with another person. Good relationship and communication skills are needed to enjoy real intimacy.

REFLECTIONS AND EXERCISES

1. MODELLING   Reflect on your family model. This is an exploration of your past, NOT a blaming exercise. It will provide some understanding of the attitudes and behaviours that you have now. Write in your journal what you can recollect about the following aspects of your parents' communication.

   • How did your parents speak to each other?
   • Did they show respect, or put each other down?
   • How well did they listen to each other, and to you?
   • To what degree did they talk openly about their feelings?
   • To what extent did they show affection to each other, or to you?
   • How did they settle disagreements and deal with anger?
   • Did either of your parents manipulate each other, or you, in any way?

   These reflections may take some time, but persistence will be rewarded by insight. When you have finished, examine your present behaviour in terms of the above questions, with someone who knows you well. Can you see any connection with your modelling? Are there things you would like to change? Share your findings with your partner or friend.

2. CHILDHOOD   Think back to your childhood. Can you identify things that hurt you, such as rejection or abuse by older people?

   • Write about them in your journal. Are you still carrying any grief, anger, resentment or bitterness that resulted from these traumas?
   • What would help you to deal with these issues? Would you find it helpful to talk them through with

a counsellor, your partner or a close friend? Have you considered asking for prayer about them?

3. What positive memories do you have of your childhood, such as: quality time spent with parents; being listened to, affirmed and encouraged; told that you were loved or special.

   • These are wonderful memories. Record them in your journal and think about them. Thank God for them.
   • If you are part of a group, you might like to share these.

4. DEFENCE MECHANISMS   Read again the section in this chapter on defence mechanisms. Can you identify any processes of denial, rationalisation, projection or repression operating in your life? It may be helpful to talk this over with someone who knows you well and who would be prepared to help you take an honest look at your life. It is not easy to get in touch with 'blind spots'.

5. DIFFERENCES   How do you handle differences between you and your friends or partner? Do they threaten you? Do you avoid thinking about them, or talking about them with him/her? Do you see them as things which enhance or damage your relationship?

   • Are there peculiarities *in you* that might annoy others?
   • How could you maximise the benefit of the differences in a relationship?
   • Reflect on these in your journal, then discuss them with your friend/partner.

6. COMMUNICATION SKILLS   How effective are you as a communicator? Ask someone who knows you well and would give you an honest answer.

   • Check through the skills listed in chapters two and six and see how you measure up in these areas.
   • How could you improve your communication skills?

SEVEN

KEYS TO INTIMACY

If you want to be loved, love.
                    Seneca, 4 BC to AD 65[1]
Speak the truth in love.
                    Paul, c. AD 64[2]

The last chapter described some of the blocks to developing intimate relationships. These are present in each of us to some degree, as it is unlikely that anyone deals fully with all of their 'baggage'. If we waited until this process was complete before starting to reach out to others, we would never have any close friends! However, to be aware of the blocks and baggage, and to be *working on them*, clears the way for us to develop intimacy. Close friends can help each other in this process. In this chapter we explore some essential ingredients of an intimate relationship.

KEYS TO INTIMACY

1. Commitment

Priorities
Experiencing intimacy starts with a desire for it and commitment to work at it. Because the development of intimacy takes time, intimate relationships have to be a priority in our lives or they will never happen. We do not *find* time for intimacy, we have to *make* time for it. In our Western, achievement-driven society time is our most precious commodity, because time means money. We spend time

on those things we consider important. If work success is our priority, that is where we will spend time and energy. If relationship with family and friends is of more value, we will sacrifice other goals for this.

This has been a battle for me (John) as I started out in life very goal-oriented. In our medical programme in Papua New Guinea I set goals to ensure efficiency and to prove to myself and others that I was a success. I engaged in medical and epidemiological research in my 'spare time', to improve the effectiveness of our work. At the end of twenty-one years I had amassed a large amount of data, which I planned to use towards a PhD thesis.

On returning to New Zealand in 1976, I was challenged about my goals. I realised that my teenage family needed a father, not a remote academic living in the house. Agnes needed a husband and not a research worker. 'People matter more than things'; relationships are more important than degrees. So I decided to give away my ambitious dream and obtained part-time employment in order to have time free for people.

But the battle is still there. Almost every week I have to evaluate my programme to see if enough time has been set aside for my relationships with God, my wife, my family and others. Old patterns die slowly, and a people-oriented value system flows against the tide of the society in which we live. Keeping a journal helps me to be accountable to the priorities I have set. We will not know intimacy in our lives unless we are committed to it. Of course, for an intimate relationship to develop, two people must share this priority.

Mutual Desire
If two people desire an intimate relationship it has to be by mutual consent and planning, and it is not possible to have a close relationship unless both want it. Two friends or partners rarely have exactly the same need for intimacy. Often one will desire it more than the other and in different ways. This has to be openly discussed and negotiated. In

our own relationship we had to work hard at this because our needs for intimacy were different.

I (Agnes) grew up in a close, extended family. My life revolved around a network of relationships which were important to me. John became independent at an early age. He liked people but did not need them. When we met, we both desired to be together, but my needs for intimacy were greater than his. For many years I was unable to talk about it and he was unaware of the problem. In the years when our children needed most mothering, that became a substitute for the intimacy that was lacking in my relationship with John. We had a lot of work to do to find a comfortable balance between intimacy and autonomy. As the years passed, I became aware of the need for more autonomy and John grew in his desire for intimacy.

One way of encouraging growth and change is to *focus on the future* rather than the past, on possibilities not problems. Ask questions like: 'How could we improve the quality of our relationship?', or, 'What would our relationship be like if there was more intimacy?'. Using your imagination to focus on the future will help to identify things that limit your present experience of intimacy. This is a process we use ourselves, as well with people we counsel.[3]

Autonomy

In a healthy relationship there is an ebb and flow between autonomy and intimacy, independence and inter-dependence. Intimacy is an intense experience, and we cannot be intimate all the time. All relationships need space where each can have time to breathe, relax and grow. We can then bring to our intimacy the fruits of our autonomy. Kahlil Gibran expressed this healthy tension:

Let there be spaces in your togetherness.
And let the winds of the heavens dance between you.
Love one another, but make not a bond of love:
Let it rather be the moving sea between the shores of your souls.

Fill each other's cup but drink not from one cup.
Give one another of your bread but eat not from the
same loaf.
Sing and dance together and be joyous, but let each
one of you be alone, even as the strings of the lute are
alone though they quiver with the same music.
Give your hearts, but not into each other's keeping.
For only the hand of Life can contain your hearts.
And stand together, yet not too near together:
For the pillars of the temple stand apart,
And the oak tree and the cyprus grow not in each
other's shadow.[4]

Balance

The balance between intimacy and autonomy is not the
same in all relationships, and it varies at different times
in the same relationship. Friends and partners must find
the balance that is right for them, and frequently need to
check out with each other how they feel about their level of
intimacy. Consider Figure 14. We start off as strangers and
become friends. Moving into a close relationship involves
different degrees of overlap.

Some people, especially early in a relationship, become
what family therapists call 'enmeshed'. Their overlap is
too intense and smothering. The drive for this usually
comes from one partner and the other colludes, until she/he
becomes suffocated and may opt out. It is often hard to
change this dynamic to a more healthy one without dis-
rupting the relationship.

This is because enmeshment usually involves a process
known as *symbiosis*. In nature, this refers to two organisms
that not only live together but are necessary for each other's
survival. Examples of this in human relationships are: a
dominant person living with an overly submissive partner;
a 'rescuer' supporting someone who sees him/herself as
a 'victim'; a quiet person hiding behind someone who is
gregarious and talkative. On the surface it may seem that
they are suited to one another. But the danger is that they

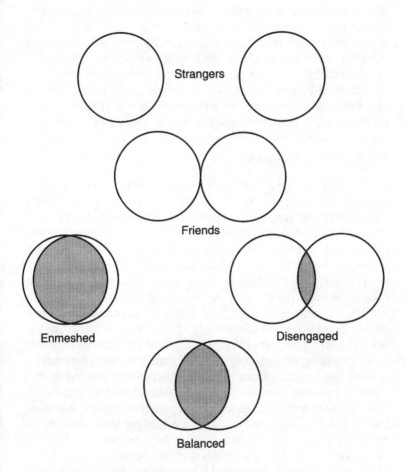

Figure 14. Variations in intimacy

can feed each other's neurosis and prevent growth and change. The arrangement may seem convenient, but deep down each person would like things to be different.

At the other end of the scale, friends or couples may have little overlap and can be described as being 'disengaged'.

This is fine if that is what they *both* want, but often one partner is dissatisfied with this level of intimacy. Sometimes neither of them want this but they do not have the communication skills to do anything about it. Healthy intimacy is a balanced relationship, where there is closeness but both partners also have sufficient autonomy. The degree of overlap is not constant, and the amount of intimacy varies. When two people are stuck at one or other extreme, their intimacy needs are not likely to be met.

2. Other-Centredness

During my nursing training I (Agnes) met up with a fellow student and over a period of time we became friends. What impressed me was her ability to be there for others, even when it was inconvenient. She did not do it to impress others but just to be friendly, loving and caring. This was because she *was* a giving and accepting person. She cared deeply for people because she was other-centred. Another colleague was quite the opposite. She seldom did more than the bare minimum for patients in the course of her duties. She was brilliant academically, but showed little feeling for others, or for anything which did not advantage her. Self-centredness certainly did not win her many friends!

Nothing spoils intimacy faster than self-centredness, or a desire to gratify personal needs at the expense of others. We have worked with many couples where this is their stumbling block. Each partner is hurting, not having their own needs met, and each sees the other as the selfish one. The dynamic is unlikely to change until both start applying the golden rule: 'Do to others what you would have them do to you.'[5] In his book, *Getting the Love You Want*, Harville Hendricks shows how this principle of deliberately setting out to please one another often helps couples move away from their stuck positions of selfishness and start changing the way they relate.[6]

Preoccupation with self may not always be deliberate selfishness. For example, people who struggle with a sense of low self-esteem carry around a pain inside them all the time: 'Am I good enough? Will I be rejected as I have been in the past? What does he/she think of me? How should I react to look good in this situation?' If these thoughts fill my mind, it is difficult to focus on you. If we both struggle with this issue, we multiply our problems.

On the other hand, people with a good sense of self-worth can forget about themselves and reach out to others. They can more readily focus on the needs and interests of others because they are not preoccupied with themselves.[7] There are three essential aspects of other-centredness:

Love

Other-centredness implies loving unconditionally. This means that friends and lovers make a commitment like: 'I'm going to love you and there is nothing you can do which will stop me!' The New Testament uses the Greek word, *agape*, when talking about this kind of loving (see p 31).[8] 'Agape-love' is not easy, and does not come naturally. It is God's way of loving. In our own relationship we are aware of the need to draw on his love and strength to be able to love each other this way consistently.[9]

Giving

True intimacy grows in an atmosphere of giving rather than receiving. This does not deny the fact that when we give we are likely to receive, but our giving is not to be based on a calculated return. Give anyway!

In the context of relationships, Jesus stated this profound truth:

> Give, and it will be given to you. A good measure, pressed down, shaken together and running over, will be poured into your lap. For with the measure you use, it will be measured to you.[10]

Intimacy grows in the climate of uninhibited generosity. What I have and who I am is a gift I offer you. There is always a risk that my gift will not be received, or may even be rejected.

But unless I take this risk, you will never know the extent of my desire for closeness. If that gift is reciprocated we can experience intimacy that transcends friendship.

Acceptance
In the last chapter we saw that differences between people are attractive initially but later can block their intimacy. True acceptance of others is not easy. Acceptance means valuing other people's uniqueness and affirming their differences as being right for them. It is easier to accept others when we experience acceptance from others. *Mutual* acceptance is a beautiful bond which strengthens intimacy.[11]

Acceptance

To know acceptance
is to know the ecstatic freedom to be me
when you're around;
that not an ounce of acting is necessary
to earn your affections.

To know acceptance
is to hang limp in the arms of your company,
to dare to lift the wraps
on both my hopes and fears with equal ease,
and know I will not be judged for being human.

To know acceptance
is to know weightlessness,
a place in which to stretch . . . grow . . . and become,
a place of rest from
those amongst whom I must stay on guard.

It is only in the haven of your acceptance
that I feel safe enough to be loved,
and without love,
all I can expect to grow
is older.

Graeme Packer[12]

3. Self-Revelation

The ability to share yourself and reveal who you are to another person does not come naturally to adults. It is an art to be learned. Many people go through life without developing this skill, and consequently never experience satisfying intimacy in their relationships. But we all have a deep desire to know and be known. Self-revelation can be at different levels and in a range of different areas.

For two people to really know each other they need to be able to disclose their hurts and fears as well as hopes and dreams; their weaknesses and struggles as well as strengths and victories. They are not afraid to discuss moral and spiritual values openly. They can communicate comfortably at a feeling level.

We have frequently seen a tremendous release when people reveal the pain, hurt and feelings that they have carried around for many years. It frees them to grow as individuals and in their relationships. There is a lot of evidence to support the fact that self-disclosure promotes physical health. Certainly the reverse is true. People who bottle up grief, repress childhood memories of emotional, sexual or physical abuse, or hold on to bitterness and unforgiveness are much more prone to illness. Not releasing these things lowers the immune response and the defence mechanisms of the body against illness.

Two essentials in this process of self-disclosure are being able to remove my masks and sharing feelings appropriately.

Removing Masks

Wearing masks was identified in chapter six as one of the blocks to intimacy. Lowering or removing our masks makes us vulnerable, but intimacy grows when two people risk this degree of openness. Masks are hard to remove, even if we want to do so. One person expressed it this way:

Don't be fooled by me or by the face I wear, for I have

a thousand masks and none of them are me. I give the impression that I'm secure, that confidence is my game and coolness my name, that the water's calm and I'm in command. But, don't believe me, please! Beneath dwells the real me in confusion, fear and loneliness. I panic at the thought of my weakness and fear being exposed. That's why I frantically create masks to hide behind, to shield me from the glance that knows. But such a look is precisely my salvation, if it is followed by acceptance and love.

And so begins the parade of masks, and my life becomes a front. I chatter to you in suave tones of surface talk. I tell you everything that is really nothing, and nothing of what is everything. So don't be fooled when I go through my routine. Please listen carefully and try to hear what I'm *not* saying. I dislike hiding, honestly! I'd really like to be genuine and spontaneous with you, and you can help me. With your sensitivity, sympathy and the power of your understanding, you can breathe life into me.

I want you to know how important you are to me. You can help me remove my mask behind which I tremble. So please don't pass me by. It will not be easy for you, because I fight the very thing I cry out for. But love is stronger than masks, and in this lies my hope. Please help me remove my masks with firm but gentle hands.

Who am I, you may wonder?

I am someone you know very well.

I am every man or woman you meet.

Author unknown

Revealing Feelings

Behind every mask is a real person, and intimacy can only develop between real people. You will never know who I am until you know *my feelings*. I can never know you unless you reveal to me who you really are. My feelings are me, whereas facts, ideas and thoughts are from outside. There are many facts that we have made our own, and we all have values that we believe in. So in that sense they are ours, but we were not born with them. We were born with emotions and a capacity to develop a range of feelings that are specific to each of us. 'Feelings are as unique as our fingerprints.'[13] Working through Exercise 5 at the end of this chapter with someone will show you the validity of this statement.

No two people experience the same feeling in the same way. So if I want to know you and you want to know me, we must discover each other's uniqueness. Feelings are the raw materials with which we build close relationships. As John Powell says: 'If I don't know your feelings, I don't know you, and if I don't know you, how can I love you?' To develop intimacy it is essential that we are able to share at a feeling level.

Why it is so Difficult to Share Feelings

Many factors in our society militate against the development of intimacy and some of these were discussed in chapter four. Because sharing feelings is the means by which we build intimacy with another person, these same factors ensure that our feelings are usually kept well hidden. This is particularly true for males in our 'stiff-upper-lip', 'keep-it-close-to-your-chest', 'big-boys-don't-cry' culture. Most men find it difficult to acknowledge a feeling. Conversations between males seldom include feelings, and women often complain that they do not know what husbands or male friends feel.

Males are supposed to be in control. They are usually more comfortable giving information rather than asking for it, and are unlikely to admit to feelings of uncertainty or confusion. Male 'control' covers the need to repress feelings. Most men are embarrassed to cry or show tenderness in public.

Fear is another emotion which must be controlled, so a man is unlikely to admit to fear or insecurity. Even expressions of joy or happiness are regarded with suspicion by many men, except perhaps at a sporting event!

Some men are unable to admit that they are discouraged or depressed, so will often express a confident view in situations where they feel the opposite. The only feeling which many men can express spontaneously is anger. This may not be a nice feeling, but it is not 'un-male' to be angry.

Most men spend the major part of their lives in a work environment where expressing feelings is inappropriate. Covering up feelings with a 'mask' is understandable in a competitive work situation, but is totally inappropriate in a setting of intimacy. As a result of this gender conditioning, the majority of men have a lot of mates but few intimate friends. Hiding feelings is something boys learn from their fathers, and this modelling is reinforced by the cultural norms just described.

I (John) grew up in a loving home. I learned a lot of good values from my father, but I also concluded that to be a strong person I had to hide my feelings. I vividly remember being with him when he received the telegram to say that my brother had been killed. Harry flew a Spitfire in the Battle of Britain and was shot down over Holland. As my dad read the news, he was very moved, but did not cry. That day, at twelve years of age, I learned that if I wanted to be strong like my father I should not cry. It was another thirty years before I was able to cry again.

The thing that helped me get in touch with and express my feelings is the model Jesus gave us. He was a feeling person and expressed the whole range of feelings in a healthy way. His biographers recorded his joy, sadness, compassion, anger, tiredness, loneliness, and disappointment.[14] He knew deep depression in the Garden of Gethsemane: 'My soul is overwhelmed with sorrow to the point of death.'[15] He cried at the grave of a friend, despite the fact that he was about to bring Lazarus back to life again.[16] If the Man Jesus expressed feelings, why should I try to hide mine?

Women are permitted in our culture to have feelings and express them, though men often regard this as a weakness.

Some women who operate in a male work environment adopt male attitudes towards controlling feelings. Women who are married to men who cannot share feelings may also find it difficult to share theirs. This is because when they do so, their feelings may be devalued or dismissed. People who cannot share their own feelings usually are unable to accept the feelings of others. Here are some guidelines for both sharing and receiving feelings.

How to Share Feelings
I own the feeling and accept responsibility for it
The first step is to identify the feeling and acknowledge it. A feeling arises in response to a stimulus or event, either from outside or within my mind. Identification of the feeling happens this way:

I experience an event or stimulus
↓
My body responds physiologically
↓
I interpret this arousal and decide what emotion I am feeling
↓
I experience this emotion

This is called *cognitive labelling* of emotions[17] and is something we all do. For example:

a) I notice someone staring at me
b) My heart beat increases
c) I could interpret this response in a variety of ways, and I choose one:
   - *pleasure*, because someone is interested in me
   - *fear*, because of unexpected attention from a stranger
   - *frustration*, because I was hoping to remain unobserved
d) I experience the feeling that I have decided is appropriate.

The next step is to acknowledge to myself that I have the feeling and that this feeling is *mine*. People who have repressed their feelings for many years find this difficult.

Owning a feeling also means taking responsibility for it. Nobody can *give* you a feeling. You may be angry, frustrated or disappointed with others, but these are your feelings in response to what they are doing. No one can *make* you angry or sad. No one can *make* you happy or contented. God has created us unique individuals who are responsible for our own lives, behaviour and feelings.

To blame someone else for my feelings puts me at the mercy and whim of another and takes away my dignity as a human being. This is a fundamental principle in dealing with feelings. To know that my feeling is mine and not given to me by someone else sets me free to take control of it. It frees me from the 'blame game', which is the first recorded human defence mechanism.[18] It empowers me to take responsibility for my actions before God.

I tell you my feeling honestly
If intimacy is dependent on mutual sharing of feelings, I need to learn how to do this in a way that is safe for both of us. You cannot guess my feelings or really know them.[19] You may observe my body language that suggests I have a strong feeling, but as was pointed out in chapter two, all messages need to be checked out. The only way you will know my feeling is if I tell you about it honestly.

Paul gives us the key to doing this in one of the greatest essays on relationships in all literature, Ephesians 4:

Speaking the truth in love
we will in all things GROW UP
into him who is the Head, that is, Christ.

Here, in verse 15, he is talking about 'growing up' or becoming mature in our relationship with Christ. But it is the *key to any relationship*.

Intimacy means sharing the truth of who I am in a loving way. In terms of expressing feelings, the truth is how I feel right now but I need to tell you about it in a way that builds our relationship and does not destroy it. In verse 25 he states again that if we want oneness we must 'speak truthfully to one another'. An honest sharing of my feelings could be hurtful to you unless I do it in a loving way, so I need to own my truth without blaming you for it.

I choose wording and timing carefully

The words we use are crucial. As we grow up it is easy to acquire destructive ways of expressing ourselves. For example, we commonly say: 'You make me angry' or 'You upset me', when the truth is: 'I am angry with you', or 'I feel upset when you do/say . . .'. It may sound simplistic, but just making an 'I' statement rather than a 'you' statement is often all that is required.

Now the other person does not have to defend him/herself. The door is open to meaningful exchange when I make myself vulnerable, own my feelings, and tell you about them without blaming you for them. The situation may still be uncomfortable for a while, especially if my feeling is in response to something you have said or done. But if you are not being blamed for it, there is less pressure and you can respond without defensiveness or aggression.

Timing in expressing feelings is also important, and the rule is as soon as possible. Sometimes it may not be appropriate to share the feeling immediately. Others may be present, something else may be more pressing, the other person may be tired or upset, or the feeling may be so intense that we need some time to gain control.

Paul gave a useful rule of thumb with regard to timing in verse 26: do not go to bed with feelings that have not been dealt with. If I go to bed angry or with any other strong feeling, I will be even less likely to deal with it the next day. So the feeling will be relegated to a growing pool of discomfort or bitterness. I will also have lost the opportunity to use the feeling to enhance intimacy.

I share feelings to build relationships

Feelings can be expressed in a hurtful way, and when they are 'dumped' on others relationships are destroyed. Paul ends his teaching on communication and good relationships with:

> Be completely humble and gentle; be patient, bearing
> with one another in love . . . Be kind and compassion-
> ate to one another, forgiving each other, just, as in
> Christ God forgives you.

Misunderstandings and conflicts would not last long if we put these principles into practice.

How to Receive Feelings

Nobody will risk sharing feelings unless they know that they will be received appropriately. If your feelings are unlikely to be treated with respect it is safer to keep them to yourself. The skills of sharing and receiving feelings go together, and people who are poor at expressing feelings will probably be insensitive to the feelings of others.

One reason why many men find it hard to share their own feelings is because they do not know how to receive other's feelings. Often males want *to do something* about the feelings that others share with them. This is because men see themselves as 'problem-solvers' in society; their role is to fix things and provide solutions. Thus if someone, especially a woman, shares a feeling with a man, he will be tempted to explain the feeling or even to try and take it away. At other times he may just ignore her feeling, because he does not know what to do.

The worst sin of all is to tell your friend or partner that she should not have that feeling. This will add *guilt* to the feeling. Yet how often we hear statements like: 'You shouldn't feel like that!' 'Don't feel sad, it will be all right' 'There's no need to be afraid'. When feelings are ignored or belittled, the feeler feels put down. If feelings are respected and valued, the feeler feels significant. If feelings are acknowledged and validated, the feeler is affirmed.

The way to receive feelings is simply *to listen* to them. Listening is loving. Listening means: 'What you say is important to me, therefore you are important to me.'

The listener does not have to be able to identify with or experience the feeling, merely to listen to it and accept it as real for the other person. This validates the feeling. The listener can attempt to feel that feeling too but may not be fully successful. Showing empathy in this way is affirming for the person who is sharing the feeling.

This is an aspect of our relationship that I (Agnes) struggled with for a long time. John was not only a typical male who wanted to explain my feelings away, he is also a doctor, and so had an urge to take them away. But I did not want my feelings fixed. Nor did I appreciate being treated as a patient! All I wanted was for him to listen to me, and by this to show that he cared.

I knew he could not fully understand my feelings. Sometimes I do not understand them myself. But when we learned how to listen to one another's feelings, things changed. John no longer took responsibility for them, which was not his job anyway. Once he really heard my feelings, they lost their power, and I was better able to deal with them.

We have developed a *contract* for dealing with feelings in relationships based on one described by David and Vera Mace.[20] A contract is an agreement between two people. We have shared this contract over the years with many couples, and encouraged them to sign and date the contract, and place it in a prominent place in their home for a while. The whole family can use this process to deal with feelings. The feelings contract has four simple steps:

---

1. I *own* my feelings (to myself)
2. I will *share* my feelings with you
3. I will *not clobber* you with my feelings
4. I ask you to *help me* with my feelings

Own the Feelings
To own my feelings means to acknowledge them and identify that I really do feel them. People who are used to burying their feelings find this difficult. Owning a feeling means more than acknowledging it. Part of identifying a

feeling is to explore the reason for it and often the feeling
behind it. For example, anger is always a secondary feeling.
Behind anger lies fear, sadness, insecurity, frustration, or
other feelings which also must be dealt with. Part of owning
a feeling is the willingness to take responsibility for it: 'This
feeling is mine and I will deal with it properly.'

Share Feelings
We have described how to share feelings and how to receive
them. These skills need practice because although they are
simple they are not easy. A contract like this one provides a
safety net in that both partners have agreed to learn how to
share their feelings together. When we were first married and
Agnes asked me how I was feeling, I did not hesitate to tell
her. The problem was I could only identify two feelings: 'Fine'
or 'OK'. This left her frustrated, especially when she could see
from my body language that I was not fine or OK. I was 'feelings illiterate' and had to develop a new vocabulary as well as
the skill of sharing feelings. There are literally hundreds of feeling words, and we spent many hours learning to talk feelings
and discovering how we differed in our experience of them.

No Clobbering
'Clobbers' refer to ways in which we can hurt one another
in relationships. Some typical ones are: ignoring the other's
feeling; refusing to discuss it; belittling the other for having
the feeling, as if it were a weakness. Another way is to use
the knowledge of the other's feeling to assert superiority
or power over him/her . . . 'There you go again, you are
stupid to feel like that.' Small wonder that people are scared
to share their feelings! But the price of hiding our feelings
from those who are close to us is loss of intimacy. This
contract provides a framework to identify our mistakes,
apologise and start afresh.

Help Each Other to Share Feelings
Helping each other with feelings means listening to them
creatively. There is no need to say anything, except perhaps

to ask clarifying questions or reflect back what we understand the other is saying. But analysis, passing judgement, or giving advice have no place in this process. This fourth stage is the *relationship-building* part of the contract, and two people feel much closer when they are able to share their feelings and help each other with them. This skill needs regular practice. People who want to maintain intimacy need to share feelings at least on a daily basis. We describe this more fully in chapter nine in talking about intimacy in marriage.

Summary

Intimacy in relationships does not happen automatically and needs to be worked for. Intimacy thrives when both friends are other-centred, with a desire to give rather than merely receive. They must also be able to share themselves with each other in a mutual process of revealing and receiving feelings.

REFLECTIONS AND EXERCISES

1. FOCUS ON THE FUTURE   Picture a significant relationship of yours *as if* it was as intimate as you would wish it to be.

   • Explore this in your journal. What would be happening that is not happening now? What changes might achieve the desired result?
   • Share your ideas with that person. The model of overlapping circles (Figure 14) may help.

2. PRIORITIES   Make a list of goals or things that are important to you, e.g. career, marriage. family, sport, TV, travel, health, hobbies, relationships with certain people, a growing relationship with God.

   • Write them down first in a *horizontal* order. Then place them in a *vertical* list in order of priority.

   Now reflect in your journal on the following questions:

   a) Is developing intimate relationships high enough on this list?
   b) If the vertical order of goals represents my *priorities*, does it also represent where I spend my time, money and effort?
   c) If there is a mismatch between my stated priorities and what is actually happening, what can I change?

3. OTHER-CENTREDNESS   Write in your journal an assessment of how other-centred you are in a relationship with someone, in terms of:

   a) The level of unconditional love you have for that person.
   b) How much you give rather than take in this relationship.
   c) How well you accept the other person, especially their qualities that you find difficult.

- If the other person has done this exercise too, discuss together what you have both written.

4. MASKS   Identify masks that you wear. Re-reading the section on some typical masks (chapter six) could be helpful.

    Then answer these questions in your journal:

    a) Why do I wear this mask, e.g. to hide, impress, express how I would like to be, enlist support, avoid dealing with unresolved issues.
    b) Do I still need to wear it, at least in my intimate relationships?
    c) What would be the advantages of not wearing this mask?
    d) What would help me to remove it?

5. EXPLORING FEELINGS   Each person feels a feeling in their own unique way. To demonstrate this, and to help you have a better understanding of each other's feelings, expand feeling words in the following way. Take fear, for example. This is how one person experiences fear:

    When I feel *afraid* I feel uncertain,
    When I feel *uncertain* I feel confused,
    When I feel *confused* I feel insecure,
    When I feel *insecure* I feel lonely,
    When I feel *lonely* I feel *sad*.

Another person experiences fear like this:

    When I feel *afraid* I feel panicky,
    When I feel *panicky* I feel out of control,
    When I feel *out of control* I feel helpless
    When I feel *helpless* I feel weak,
    When I feel *weak* I feel *useless*.

This shows that two people can experience what they might assume is the same feeling in different ways. Each uses a different spectrum of feelings to describe fear. One ends up feeling sad and the other useless.

• Work through a number of feeling words with some-one else and discover how different or similar your feelings are.

PART TWO

THE DEVELOPMENT OF INTIMACY

In the last three chapters we focus on the development of intimacy in three specific areas.

Chapter 8
Singleness provides many opportunities to experience intimacy. It is also the best state in which to grow to maturity. We define some struggles of the single life-style, and also some advantages single people have for enjoying intimacy.

Chapter 9
Marriage provides a potentially ideal situation where two people can grow in intimacy. Unfortunately, the experience of most married people is less than their expectations. We outline how a growing intimacy in marriage is achievable, with planning and work.

Chapter 10
God designed us for intimacy with himself, and he desires friendship and intimacy with us even more than we do. Relational keys to intimacy with God are similar to those for human intimacy, and there are a range of devotional ways to develop this intimacy.

EIGHT

INTIMACY AND SINGLENESS

I actually enjoy being single!

Cliff Richard[1]

We start life experiencing intimacy. The sense of connectedness between child and mother established in the womb is gradually lost as she/he develops a sense of identity, separate from mother, by about the age of eighteen months. From then on we all experience singleness. Most people stay that way for about a quarter of a century, a third of the average life span. Others remain single throughout their lives. Some marry and then become single again through the death of their partner, or divorce.

Singleness is natural, and is not a disease for which marriage is the cure. Singles are not loose ends waiting to be tied up! Life can be equally fulfilling whether single or married, although in different ways. Singles can enjoy good relationships just as much as married people. In fact, they have opportunities to experience intimacy with a greater range of people than is possible for married people.

TYPES OF SINGLENESS

It is forty-three years since we were single. Although we remember those days quite vividly, our subsequent experience of marriage makes it harder for us to make relevant comment on this topic. However, we have interviewed a number of single men and women and discussed their experience of singleness at some depth. We have also read widely on this topic. So we present these observations with humility and a desire to be sensitive to this issue. There are a number of different types of singleness.

Circumstantial Singleness

Two out of every five adults in Western societies are single, which means there are more single adults than married couples. Churches usually contain more single than married people, yet often do not cater adequately for the needs of singles. Many single adults have not chosen to live that way. This includes those who are separated, divorced, or whose partner has died, as well as those who have never married.

Most people assume that they will marry one day and look forward to it. Some are so desperate to marry that this becomes an obsession. As the years pass and prospects of marriage recede, coming to terms with singleness may be increasingly difficult. It is hard for people who have enjoyed a satisfying marriage to adjust to being solo again, after the death of their partner or relationship breakdown.

Chosen Singleness

There are a number of reasons why people may choose to remain single. Some men and women want to enjoy the benefits of singleness and not be restricted by the responsibilities of marriage. This choice is not uncommon for people who do not have the above problems. They may live in temporary sexual relationships, but avoid long-term commitments.

Some have been so emotionally damaged as children that they cannot contemplate marriage. They may have grown up in a dysfunctional family, or were sexually abused. The resulting sense of low self-esteem and inferiority feelings can lead to a fear of intimacy. Others struggle with their sexual identity. They may be overtly homosexual and move into 'gay' relationships, or choose to remain single. Sometimes they marry in an attempt to solve their sexual identity issues. Such relationships are unlikely to be successful.

Chosen Celibacy

Some people choose a celibate lifestyle as a way of dealing with the problems described above. Others see celibacy as a calling and gift from God, as Paul did.[2] Celibacy is also seen as a valid option today for some people who do not have a Christian motivation. It must be acknowledged that certain personalities are probably more suited to the celibate lifestyle than others. People choose celibacy for a variety of reasons.

Some want to have more freedom to pursue a career or to serve God without the restriction of family responsibilities. Marriage, a legitimate option for them, is sacrificed for something they regard as more important. Jesus refers to people who have made this choice as having 'renounced marriage because of the kingdom of heaven'.[3] Paul regarded being unmarried as an advantage in the work he was called to do, especially in view of the prevailing persecution of Christians. So he recommended a single lifestyle to others,[4] and he actually considered singleness preferable to marriage.[5]

Others choose a celibate lifestyle in a religious community because they believe that this will enable them to develop a deeper relationship with God, sharing with people who have a similar commitment. One Sister said that celibacy for her was a 'love commitment to Jesus, the primary love of my life'. We have met other Christians, not in any religious community, who have also chosen celibacy with an openness and zest for life. They find fulfilment and a joy in living that many married people would long to experience.

Celibacy does not mean loss of contact with people or the absence of intimacy. In fact, it increases opportunities for both. We have a number of single friends who have rich and rewarding friendships with both single and married people, and describe some of their friendships as close and intimate. Neither does celibacy mean repression of sexuality, because our sexuality is the expression of our whole person. But to forgo genital sex and parenting involves sublimating this drive and channelling it into other areas of life. Jesus chose celibacy and lived a full, whole, rewarding life as a single person. He modelled this for us as a young man. The Apostle Paul followed the same pattern into later life.

SOME STRUGGLES OF SINGLENESS

Prejudice and Misconceptions

We live in a society where couples are the norm, whether married or not. Invitations are usually extended to a person and his/her partner. People on their own are often marginalised and regarded with suspicion, as if they are inadequate, 'gay', abnormal, or at least have a problem. It is assumed that a single man lacks initiative and a single woman is either too dominating and independent, or else weak. Many such misconceptions abound.[6] Even dividing people into 'single' or 'married' categories is not helpful socially. Unfortunately, churches often persist in separating people into these two groups, like the 'haves' and the 'have-nots'.[7]

Loneliness

We all have to deal with loneliness, and it is not confined to a single lifestyle. In chapter one we pointed out that loneliness is not solved by marriage, and that many married people experience 'living-together-loneliness'. Nevertheless, the expectation that marriage will automatically solve loneliness is common, and adds to the pain a single person may feel returning to an empty flat and a lonely bed at the end of a day. Even if we have a number of good friends, each of us longs for 'someone special who is there for me, interested in me and committed to me'.

Touch

Human beings are created with a 'skin hunger' which is only met by healthy touch. Touching heals, reduces stress and is a non-verbal way of communicating the message 'I love you . . . you're important to me'. Touch is especially important for children, but adults need it too, and many people in Western society are touch-deprived. Some married people have little touch in their lives, even though they have the opportunity.

It can be hard for singles to have their touch needs met appropriately, especially older people. Another age group with a high need for touch developmentally are adolescents, who are coping with identity confusion in the process of separating from parents. Many young adults receive minimal touch. I (John) remember giving a single man a hug after a counselling session. He told me that this was the first time he had received some caring touch since leaving home fourteen years previously.

Sexual Needs and Pressures

Single people have the same God-given sex drive and needs that married people have, and sexual needs do not switch off when a marriage ends. The message from our society is that everyone must be in a sexual relationship to be healthy. This is a lie. 'Despite what our culture tells us, sexual union is not the goal of our existence.'[8] But that does not make the problem any easier for single people, especially for Christians who are committed to celibacy.

Genital sex is only a small part of being a sexual person. Helena Wilkinson writes: 'The more we understand and give expression to our femininity or masculinity, allow our needs to be met in legitimate ways, and learn to ask when in need, the less will we be frustrated by the lack of genital sex'.[9]

Self-Preoccupation

If I live on my own, only have my own needs to think of and make most decisions without having to consult another person, it is easy to become self-preoccupied. This may not be deliberate selfishness, but there is risk of withdrawing into a 'world of one'. Of course, married people can be selfish too, but if I only have my own needs to consider, I may become self-centred without realising it. If I am not living in close quarters with someone else, I will be less aware of drifting into selfishness. Unless we recognise and confront this tendency as young adults, it will be harder to become other-centred later in life. The Scriptures warn us about the dangers of selfishness.[10]

Second-Time Singleness

So far we have mainly addressed issues of single people who have never married. For those who have been married and are solo again, through the death of their partner or divorce, the problems may be greater. They have also to deal with the grief of their loss, which may take a number of years. To lose a lifetime companion, friend and lover can feel like being reduced to half a person, and the loneliness can be intense. C.S. Lewis wrote, after his wife died:

> No one ever told me that grief felt so like fear. I am not afraid, but the sensation is like being afraid. The same fluttering in the stomach, the same restlessness, the yawning. I keep on swallowing. At other times it feels like being mildly drunk, or confused. There is a sort of invisible blanket between the world and me. I find it hard to take in what anyone says. Or perhaps hard to want to take it in. It is so uninteresting. Yet I want others about me. I dread the moments when the house is empty. If only they would talk to one another and not to me.[11]

One of the greatest compensations of a truly intimate relationship is that even when one partner dies, they both have the satisfaction of knowing that they had lived fully and loved totally. But this loss can be as great whether or not the relationship had been a good one. I (Agnes) befriended an elderly widow whose marriage had been unhappy. One day we were out walking and saw an older couple strolling along hand-in-hand. With great sadness she told me of her grief for 'the relationship I never had'.

Coming to terms with divorce can be harder than with death, because the other person is still around, and perhaps married to someone else. The separated or divorced person often feels a sense of guilt on top of their grief. This is sometimes added to by the judgemental attitude of friends, who may find it hard to cope with 'half a couple'. Solo parents can find singleness again especially hard because of parenting responsibilities, which they now have to handle on their own. A church fellowship is where second-time singles could expect to experience love and caring. We know that God is concerned about them.[12]

SOME ADVANTAGES OF SINGLENESS

The problems and pain of singleness are real, but so are the advantages. Cliff Richard gives three good reasons why he 'stays solo', in his book *Single-Minded*: 'fulfilment, freedom and friendship'.[13] He freely acknowledges the privileges and opportunities he has that others may not enjoy, but these three areas are worth considering.

Fulfilment
We have met a number of truly fulfilled single people. They are able to put all their energies into a career or calling, to a degree that would not be possible if they had marriage commitments. We have certainly found our marriage and family fulfilling, but our deepest fulfilment comes not from each other but from our faith, and a personal relationship with Christ.

One of the most significant things we are learning is *contentment*. This does not mean fatalistic tolerance, but positive acceptance of whatever circumstances come our way, and a belief that God will give the strength for any and

every situation.[14] Fulfilment and contentment is something
that both single and married people can learn.

Freedom
This is something that most married people envy in the
single lifestyle. Marriage is the only institution where two
people agree to permanently interfere with each other's
lives![15] The freedom to do what you want, when you want,
and without reference to another is something that is not
available to married people who take marriage seriously.
This freedom and independence has the inherent dangers
of self-preoccupation and self-centredness, as described
earlier. But we need not become selfish. Freedom can be
used creatively and constructively for the good of others
and to God's glory.

Friendship
On the whole, single people have a greater opportunity
for developing friendships than most married people have.
Marriage does not prevent each partner from having friends
outside of the marriage, but it does limit the opportunity
to give the time to these friendships that they may need.
A single person can more easily have close friends of
both genders. However, singles, especially widows and
divorcees are sometimes seen as a threat by married people,
who may suspect their motivation for friendship.

Singles benefit from having married friends, and couples
stand to gain much from what single friends can offer.
Entertaining a couple or a family at home can give much
pleasure to single people, as well as the reverse. Once, when
Paul was despondent and afraid, God not only encouraged
him personally, but provided a married couple to befriend
him.[16] Having friends depends on who we are, not on
whether we are married or single.

SINGLENESS AND MATURITY
The purpose of the first third or so of our lives is to develop
maturity in preparation for the rest of life, and to become

the people that we were created to be. Achieving maturity is a lifelong journey, which does not end at death for the Christian. Scott Peck wrote: 'All my life I used to wonder what I would be like when I grew up. Then, about seven years ago I realised that I was never going to grow up – that growing is an ever on-going process.'[17]

The single years can be seen either as a problem or an opportunity to focus on personal growth. As we discover who we are, understand our sexuality, develop intimacy with ourselves, deal with our 'baggage' and 'blocks', so we become capable of making close relationships. To marry before dealing with these issues makes the task of 'becoming one' much harder. A single friend of ours claims that some people marry 'because they are so poor at being single . . . People are only ready to be married when they know how to be single.'[18]

Growing to maturity means becoming *whole*. A whole person can be described as someone who is developing in all areas of life: physically, emotionally, intellectually, socially and spiritually. The human personality is most healthy when it is *balanced* and whole, and full intimacy can only be experienced by whole people. It is unhelpful to compartmentalise ourselves, but 'wholth' can be considered in five inter-relating aspects:

Physically. This means caring for the body, 'the temple of the Holy Spirit'.[19] It includes ensuring that we have adequate aerobic exercise, rest, relaxation, and a healthy diet.

Intellectual development for all of us lags far behind the potential of our minds. Intellectual closeness is important for intimacy, and means thinking together, not necessarily thinking alike. 'People learn from one another, just as iron sharpens iron.'[20]

Emotional under-development is a common limitation of wholeness. Intimacy between people will be severely restricted if they are not mature emotionally. The main determinant of intimacy is good communication, which is based on healthy intellectual and emotional sharing.

Socially. We have been created social beings.[21] An ability to relate well to a range of people of different ages, cultures and professions is evidence of maturity. If social contacts outside an intimate relationship are severely limited, it suggests that there is a degree of enmeshment.

Spiritually. Teilhard de Chardin said: 'We are not human beings having a spiritual experience, but spiritual beings having a human experience.'[22] Neglecting our spiritual development starves the most significant part of who we are, and prevents full development to wholeness. A healthy intimate relationship stimulates each other's spiritual growth. If this is not happening, the depth of the relationship is limited.

Jesus modelled this kind of wholeness. Luke describes his development as a young single person: 'Jesus grew in wisdom and stature, and in favour with God and men.'[23] He grew in 'wisdom' (intellectually and emotionally); 'and stature' (physically), 'in favour with God' (spiritually); 'and men' (socially). His biographers record that he had intimate relationships with a wide range of people, both men and women.

This process of becoming whole never stops. Healthy intimate relationships can only develop between two whole people. Part of wholeness is an awareness of how to draw safe *boundaries* in our relationships without limiting intimacy. This requires honesty and openness between two people, particularly in the emotional and sexual dimensions of their friendship.

SINGLENESS AND INTIMACY

We believe that intimacy with at least one other person is something we all need to experience and enjoy, whether single or married. It is our birthright. We have been created for intimacy. It is important to be working on developing the skills of intimacy before moving into a close relationship. These abilities do not come naturally, they have to be developed. Getting married does not give us intimacy skills, it merely reveals whether or not we have them! While growing up, it is more important to focus on *becoming* the right person than on *finding* the right partner.

The single years are not just a vacuum between loneliness and intimacy. They provide time and opportunity to develop intimate relationships with ourselves, others and God. Here is how two successful single women describe their experience: 'You don't have to be married to be happy. You just have to be alive.'[24] 'The ultimate source of satisfaction is to be found with the only Partner who can ever know us completely and love us unconditionally – God.'[25]

Summary

Singleness is a normal, natural human condition. It is possible to live a fulfilled, whole, satisfying life as a mature person whether we are single or married. The single lifestyle has particular problems and challenges, but so does marriage. Both states also have distinct advantages. Paul defines the key to a rewarding life this way: 'I have learned the secret of being content in any and every situation.'[26]

REFLECTIONS AND EXERCISES

1. EVALUATION   Draw up a balance sheet of your life in terms of singleness.[27] List positive and negative aspects of being single. Acknowledging both the advantages and disadvantages helps to obtain a more balanced picture. This does not alter the circumstances but may change the way you view them.

2. FRIENDSHIP   List how many close or intimate friends you have. Grade them in descending order of closeness. Try to identify what it is which makes you feel close to each of them.

   • How many of them are single, married, male or female? Is it easier for you to relate to any one of those four groups. If so, why?
   • In what ways could you deepen your relationship with any of those on your list?

3. STRUGGLES   Do you have difficulty with any of the issues listed in the section 'Some Struggles of Singleness' (pp 156–159)?

   • Consider the value of forming a small group with a few others who may be facing similar issues, in order to talk about them and support one another.

4. WHOLENESS   What progress are you making in becoming a whole person? Draw a circle like this and shade in the segments to represent how well you think you have developed in each of the five areas of wholeness.

   • Discuss this with a friend, or your group, to obtain objective feed-back from others.

5. THE CHURCH   How well are single people catered for in your church? Are they integrated into the life and leadership of the fellowship? Are singles singled out as a separate group, or made to feel a normal part of the family?

- Think of creative ways that single members of your congregation could be made to feel more at home. Work on this in your small group, or call together a few people for a 'brain-storming' session.

NINE

INTIMACY IN MARRIAGE

Two are better than one.[1]

H uman beings are created for intimacy with each other, whether married or single. But coupleness provides an ideal environment for developing intimacy in depth. Marriage is an example of synergy, where the result is more than the sum of the two equal parts: 'Two are better off than one, because together they can work more effectively.'[2] Intimacy takes time, and a long-term committed relationship is an opportunity for two people to experience a growing, developing, maturing closeness and inter-dependence. We all start life totally *dependent* on others and grow towards *independence*, hopefully by the time we are young adults. Only then are we ready for *inter-dependence*

ONENESS

Growth towards intimacy is the goal of marriage. This process is implied in the earliest recorded statement about marriage: 'A man leaves his father and mother and cleaves to his wife, and they become one flesh.'[3] (See Figure 15.) This profound statement implies three stages of developing intimacy in marriage.

Leaving

Marriage starts when two people leave their home of origin and the *authority* of their parents. This implies not only a physical leaving but also a psychological and emotional break from the past. The 'umbilical cord' to parents must be severed. This does not mean rejecting or abandoning parents and family. Rather, when the leaving is complete, children can develop a better adult-to-adult relationship with their parents than if they had not left home emotionally.

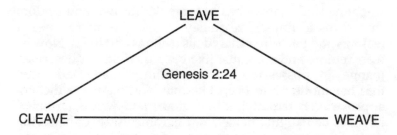

Figure 15. God's blueprint for marriage

As was described in chapter six, our childhood modelling is powerful and determines much of our behaviour in later life. People growing up in homes where healthy intimacy is clearly modelled have a distinct advantage when it comes to developing intimacy in their own marriages. Those who had a poor model in childhood find intimacy more difficult, even though they may desire it.

The model of marriage that we see in our early years is imprinted on our subconscious. Before marriage, people are more free to choose their behaviour, even in de facto relationships. But after marriage, we tend to 'act married' in the way we saw our parents relate. It is partly due to this subconscious psychological mechanism, but also to a tendency to take each other for granted now. Some couples have commented to us that they were aware of a change in their partner's behaviour right from their wedding day! This is one reason why it is a common experience for people who live together first to have more problems *after* they get married than they had before.

James and Joanne had been living together for three years.

They chose to have a 'trial run' to see if they were compat-
ible before committing themselves to marriage. These were
happy years, relatively free from conflict. They now wanted
to start a family, so decided to marry. A few months later
they came to us for counselling because they were having
frequent quarrels. They both complained that the other one
had changed.

Joanne said, 'James has become withdrawn and seldom
shared his feelings.' Previously he showed interest in her
feelings and had often shared his feelings and ideas. Now he
was 'remote and cold, just like his father'. James described
Joanne as 'possessive and controlling'. Joanne admitted
that her mother had been like that. Although she did not
approve of her mother's behaviour, and was determined
never to be like that herself, she became aware of behaving
that way at times.

They both came to realise that they were following
patterns they had observed as children. As adults they
were now free to behave differently, but found it difficult
to unlearn subconscious childhood 'scripts'.[4] But once they
recognised them, they were able to learn more satisfying
ways of relating.

It is well known that people usually choose a partner who
resembles the parent of the opposite sex. The things they
like in their mate are things they liked about their father
or mother. But researchers have found that we may also
subconsciously choose a partner who has characteristics
that we do not like, which we also saw in a parent.
Subconsciously, this represents a second chance to deal
with 'unfinished business' from our childhood.[5]

Each person is unique and therefore each couple is
unique. If a couple is to experience intimacy in their
marriage they must have a good look at the models
they brought with them. This is not a blaming exercise
but a helpful awareness process. There is no room for two
models in the same marriage. It is like trying to run a
committee meeting with two different agendas that have
not even been tabled!

Both partners have to decide on the pattern that is right for them in their relationship. This will be made up of some things from his model and some from hers, plus values that they have learned from others. Even if they each come from a home where they saw excellent marriages operating, neither parental model would be exactly right for them because their marriage is different.

Cleaving

This old English word means to be joined together or literally, 'glued together', or 'united to' (NIV). It refers to a committed relationship, based on love and good communication, enabling them to discover and understand each other. Effective communication is the basis of all successful relationships, and makes possible the goal of intimacy.

Weaving

'One flesh', in this definition of marriage, refers not only to sexual fulfilment but to becoming one emotionally and spiritually; one in goals and direction. The Hebrew word translated 'one flesh' has the sense of two lives intertwined like the warp and woof of cloth. This weaving process produces a new and beautiful tapestry, different from every other relationship. Each day they should be more married than they were the day before. If two people are growing towards wholeness, there is no end point to this exciting journey, because it is not possible to completely know someone who is developing and changing.

This definition of marriage is completed in the next sentence of the text: 'The man and his wife were both naked, and they felt no shame.' This does not merely refer to the fact that they were not wearing fig leaves yet, but implies that they had nothing to hide. Their relationship was open and transparent, without any need for masks and without shame. The first recorded consequence of sin was shame and fear.[6] While we have inherited this legacy of sin, it is possible to recapture a sense of innocence and freedom from shame, through Christ's death for us. Symbolically, we can 'return to the garden', regaining what was lost.

But what is the consequence if this weaving process does not happen? This depends on the *expectations* of both partners. If their concept of marriage is primarily that of a contractual arrangement providing a secure social and economic unit in which to raise a family, the couple may be satisfied. But if their expectation entails companionship, growing friendship and intimacy, one or both of them will be bitterly disappointed.

Traditional marriage in Western societies until about the eighteenth century has been described as: 'Popular marriage in former cultures was usually affectionless, held together by considerations of property or lineage.'[7] By contrast, most people today enter marriage with expectations of close friend-ship and intimacy. If this assumption is not met, they can feel let down and desperately lonely. This is consistent with Peplau and Perlman's definition of loneliness in chapter one. This form of loneliness in marriage has been aptly called living-together-loneliness, and is a growing phenomenon.

LIVING-TOGETHER-LONELINESS

In our counselling we have come across more lonely married people than lonely singles. The LTL syndrome, described in chapter one, is more commonly experienced by women than men. Dan Kiley coined this term and has described *five stages of LTL*: Bewilderment, Isolation, Agitation, Depression and Exhaustion.[8] These stages are accompanied by a range of feelings such as: confusion, sadness, anger, anxiety, numbness, powerlessness, worth-lessness and self-blame. These feelings reflect a process of dying inside.

Naomi was married to a well-known preacher. Dave was a 'workaholic', totally preoccupied with his work. He saw his ministry as his first priority in life, with his wife and family well behind. He kept reminding Naomi, 'You *knew* that, when we married, so you shouldn't complain!' And she seldom did. Instead, Naomi absorbed the pain and sense of rejection and blamed herself if anything went wrong. She suffered from a chronic bowel disorder and depression. Dave interpreted any episode of illness as a deliberate attempt to sabotage his work.

From being vibrant and out-going, Naomi became confused and discouraged. She felt empty, isolated, abandoned and worthless. Her occasional outbursts of anger only made her feel more guilty and depressed. She was constantly tired from the demands of a small family that she was left to bring up virtually on her own. Dave frequently told her that she was the problem. Naomi described one occasion when her husband's plane was two hours late and she fantasised that he had been killed in a crash. She was horrified that this had produced a sense of relief, not sadness. This theme recurred in her dreams.

Dave refused counselling help. 'There's nothing wrong with my marriage', he said. 'Naomi has the problem. I'm happy to pay for you to fix her.' All we could do was try to build her up, encourage her to be assertive without being aggressive, start relating to Dave as an equal, and find ways to nurture herself. Naomi's 'death wish' fantasy is not uncommon in people who experience living-together-loneliness. It reflects suicidal rather than homicidal thinking in a person who is emotionally crushed. Fortunately, there are ways of reversing loneliness in marriage, providing both partners want this.

DISCOVERING EACH OTHER

Intimacy does not happen automatically when two people live together, even if their relationship is relatively free of conflict. Intimacy flows from a desire to know each other's uniqueness. It is a common assumption that because human beings are alike, we will all experience the world in the same way. To develop intimacy with you I must lay aside that presupposition and take the time to discover how you think, feel and react. I need to really know you, to discover your 'truth', and you must discover mine.[9]

Some of the communication tools needed to do this are defined in chapters two and seven. Unless we develop the skills of creative listening and an ability to share ourselves, we will never discover each other. Many couples go through life as 'two nice people who never really know each other'. There are a number of useful techniques or tools to help people discover more about themselves and their partners. We will describe three of them.

Mutual Awareness

One way to increase awareness is to spend considerable time discussing each other's expectations of marriage, such as attitudes to work and careers, control of finance, decision making, raising children, sex, faith and many other issues. Another useful exercise is to use one of the personality tests which we described in chapter five. The more you know about each other the easier it will be to build a mutually rewarding and intimate relationship. Someone has said: 'Before marriage keep your eyes wide open, after marriage keep your eyes half shut!'

Languages of Love

Love is the 'glue' that binds two people together and nourishes intimacy. But we have all learned to love in different ways, so different in fact that they have been described as different 'languages'. This means that if we do not understand each other's 'language of the heart', we will not hear it when our partner expresses love in his or her own way. Thus we can miss the significance and intent of the other person's behaviour.

An important part of discovering each other is to *understand* each other's 'love language', and also learn to *use it*. It is a relief in a foreign country, where you do not speak the language, to have someone talk to you in your mother-tongue. Similarly, when someone uses your 'love language',

you will feel nourished. Judson Swihart defined eight different languages of love: meeting material needs; helping
each other; spending time together; meeting emotional
needs; saying it with words; saying it with touch; being
on the same side; bringing out the best in each other.[10]

Bill and Tanya were very much in love when they
married. They determined to build a good relationship,
but after two years were struggling to keep it together.
They could not understand what had gone wrong, and
each blamed the other for lack of love. We asked them to
tell us about the homes they came from. Bill grew up in
a wealthy home where he and his brother were provided
with everything they needed. Their family expressed love
by giving expensive presents for birthdays and Christmas.
His father worked hard for what they had, and ensured
that his wife never lacked for anything in the house. He
was often away from home on business.

Tanya grew up in a different setting with three sisters and
a brother. Her father also worked hard but they never had
money to spare. The way they showed love as a family was
by spending time together. The children made their own
fun and played creative games. A favourite treat was to sit
around an open fire in the evenings while dad read them
stories. As they grew up, they remained close friends and
loved to know what each other was thinking and doing.

When Bill married he wanted to provide the very best
home for Tanya, so they started out with a heavy mortgage.
He insisted on an ultra-modern kitchen, even though she
would have been content with a lot less. To pay for all this,
he had to take on an extra job which kept him busy most
evenings and weekends. What Tanya expected and wanted
most was time together. The time they did have free Bill
often slept in front of the TV, as he was so tired. Tanya
assumed that Bill did not love her any more because he
seldom spent the quality time with her now, that he had
before they were married. Bill complained that she did not
appreciate all that he was doing for her.

Each was saying 'I love you' in their own language, which

the other did not understand or appreciate. It was as if Bill was speaking French and Tanya German. They still needed to adjust their priorities and improve communication, but understanding that each was trying to say, 'I love you' and not 'I don't care about you', gave them an incentive to work through their problems. This simple insight has helped many couples.

We all speak several languages of love, but for each of us, one or two of them are likely to be more significant in terms of expressing and receiving love. Gary and Ann-Marie Ezzo have defined what they believe are the five most common languages of love.[11] These are: quality time; acts of service; physical touch and closeness; gift-giving; words of encouragement. It is helpful for each partner to arrange these five languages of love in order of preference and then compare their findings. (See exercise 4.)

This principle does not only apply to marriage, but also in learning to love children and friends. Children can feel unloved in a family simply because parents have not expressed their love in his/her primary language. Intimacy in marriage, family and between friends is greatly enhanced as we learn to express love in the way it will be best received. Sometimes we can identify others' languages of love more readily than they can, so this needs to be talked through together.

Daily Dialogue

The most important way to build intimacy in marriage is through sharing and receiving feelings, and discovering one another at an emotional level each day. The process of feelings-sharing was described in chapters two and seven. Intimacy is a learned behaviour, and sharing feelings requires *practice* through daily dialogue. Dialogue simply means a conversation between two people, but in this sense we refer to more than just talking. It is when two people share something real about themselves, opening their souls to each other.

This concept of 'emotional dialogue' is well described in John Powell's book, *The Secret of Staying in Love*. He writes, 'When I tell you my emotions and feelings I am telling you who I really am. I am giving you myself.'[12] It is possible to spend all day together with someone talking about many things without any emotional dialogue taking place. Couples can live together for years and never engage in real dialogue. This is the root cause of living-together-loneliness.

This practice of having a daily dialogue is the best way to build intimacy in marriage. It involves setting aside some time, say twenty to thirty minutes each day, to be emotionally present for each other. An auditory person might describe it as, 'Two instruments tuning up together so they can produce better harmony'. A more kinesthetic person might say, 'Feeling what it's like to be in your skin.' A visual person could call it, 'Seeing the world through your eyes.'

The daily dialogue is not a time to talk over domestic issues or solve problems. It is a time specifically set aside as a gift for each other to renew the relationship. It needs to be *quality time*, not late at night when you are nearly asleep. The best time for many couples is after the evening meal, when the children are in bed or otherwise occupied. The TV must be turned off, and it may help to take the phone off the hook as well. Early morning is preferable for some.

Affirmations

Make it a warm and happy time. A good way to start is with an exchange of affirmations, expressing what you really appreciate about each other. Then share something that is real and important about yourself: feelings, desires, dreams, insights about your relationship or life in general.

Feelings

The feeling you share could be something you are aware of right now, or felt earlier in the day, or perhaps a feeling you have about your partner or your relationship. As you become skilled in expressing feelings this becomes easier. (See chapter seven for further discussion on feelings and self-revelation.) One way of getting in touch with feelings is to play over in your mind's eye an imaginary *video of your day*, identifying feelings you had each hour or in each segment of the day.

Letters
Dialogue can be developed by writing letters to each other. These need not be lengthy epistles, maybe just one paragraph. Explore something important to you, something you want your partner to know and share about your life. This process is promoted by the Marriage Encounter Movement.[13] They call it the 10/10 exercise: 10 minutes of writing and then 10 minutes to discuss it. In writing you can express your thoughts and feelings clearly without distraction. Then, through discussion you can clarify and eliminate misunderstandings that might arise from the written message.

We suggest to couples that they write at least one letter a week. The husband could write one week and the wife the next. Give the letter to your partner in the morning to read and think about during the day. Then discuss the contents in your next dialogue session. These letters could be written in duplicate or in a note book, so that you both have a permanent record of what you have shared. This is valuable material, like gold in the bank, not to be wasted. John Powell suggests forty excellent topics for such letters, which can be used by couples as dialogue starters.[14] See also Exercise 6.

DIMENSIONS OF INTIMACY

Intimacy is like a multi-faceted diamond with many ways in which two people can develop an intimate relationship. In their book, *The Intimate Marriage*, the Clinebells explore this concept throughly.[15] No two couples will express intimacy in exactly the same way. We describe now some aspects of intimacy that are important to us.

Thinking Together

Intimacy includes what Shakespeare called 'the marriage of true minds'.[16] This means exploring new concepts together, respecting each other's intellectual capacity, and making the most of a female and male perspective on life. We enjoy reading books aloud to each other, stopping occasionally to tease out a new idea, and relate it to our own experience.

Feeling Together

Sharing at a feeling level was especially difficult for me (John), a typical male. As a couple we have had to work hard at this. But as we learned to be vulnerable and real with one another, and reveal what was happening for each of us at an emotional level, we grew in intimacy. Initially it required a conscious effort to share feelings on a regular basis. Now we feel deprived if we do not tune in, or touch base in this way at least once a day. It is food and nourishment for our relationship. A daily dialogue is as important to a marriage as a daily time of quiet and prayer is vital for a healthy spiritual life. Both processes are concerned with the same thing: building an intimate relationship.

Working Together

We find that working together in a variety of tasks enhances our intimacy profoundly. There are many ways in which a couple can work together: building a home and family; earning their livelihood; reaching out to others in a people-helping or philanthropic venture; training and study; serving God in a joint ministry. To work together closely requires acknowledging each other's gifts and talents and a healthy respect for each other's abilities.

Some couples find working together difficult. This may be due to an element of competition in their relationship. For others it could be because their communication skills are poor, or they are unable to resolve conflict. One couple we talked to were hair dressers and worked all day within a metre of each other. While this was good for their business, they were disappointed that it did not strengthen their relationship. This changed as they learned how to share at an emotional level. A strong sense of oneness and intimacy can result from sharing common tasks and goals. The ability to work together, especially under pressure, is a sensitive indicator of the strength of a marriage.

Playing Together

Learning to play together not only is good for physical health and reducing stress but it is good for relationships. To play is to celebrate life, and doing this together celebrates our common life.[17] We both came from families which modelled hard work as the norm. Life was serious. Our background included messages like: 'Don't waste time', and 'Every moment counts for eternity'. While these injunctions have a place, the Christian message is also one of joy and freedom. As a couple we had to learn how to play together, also as a family, and to relax without feeling guilty.[18]

Couples that play together stay together! Enjoying recreational pursuits together is intimacy building as well as refreshing. Outdoor activities such as tramping, cycling, sailing, swimming or just going out for a drive provide opportunities to drink from a common cup of beauty and pleasure. Sharing a creative hobby is a bonding activity. 'Wasting time' is an important part of living, and doing it together is rewarding! Sex in marriage is for fun as well as for reproduction.

Fighting Together

Intimacy and conflict might seem a contradiction in terms. It certainly felt that way to us. We both grew up in homes where neither of us had ever seen our parents express anger at one another, or resolve conflict adequately. Consequently our modelling did not prepare us to deal with anger in our own relationship. Agnes kept her anger under control most of the time, and John pretended he was not angry, hoping the uncomfortable feeling would go away if ignored.

We had both fallen for the myth: 'People who love each

other will never have conflict or be angry with one another.'
It was many years before we learned healthy ways to
process anger and use conflict constructively. 'Families
that fight together, stay together' – providing they fight
'fair' and not 'dirty'.[19]

Some cultures enjoy arguing and regard it as evidence
of being sociable or even intimate.[20] Linguistic and sociological studies have shown this to be true of Jewish people,
especially from Eastern Europe. Italians enjoy *discussione*,
what Anglo-Saxons might regard as unpleasant arguing.
People from essentially the same cultural background
can have different attitudes towards arguing, depending
on their modelling. Significant differences over this issue
cause misunderstandings in relationships.

'Never waste a good conflict!' Conflicts provide opportunities to learn something about yourself and your partner.
Healthy conflict resolution leads to personal maturity and
growth in relationships. Resolving interpersonal conflict
deepens intimacy. The reverse is also true. If conflicts
are left unresolved and buried, this leads to a growing
coldness and distance between people.[21] If people do not
know how to resolve conflict, and move into bitter fighting,
this destroys closeness. Couples who are afraid of intimacy
can resort to conflict as a means of avoiding it. One or other
picks a fight if a situation appears to be leading to intimacy.
This psychological game is called 'uproar'.[22]

The ability to resolve conflict depends largely on developing the attitudes and values outlined in chapters two
and six: love, acceptance, sincerity, giving and other-
centredness. It also requires the application of communication skills, particularly the ability to share feelings. If
both partners are able to share the feelings that lie behind
their adversarial stance *before* dealing with the facts, then
conflict resolution is much easier. Once I have exposed my
fears to the light of day, and to my best friend, I am no
longer crippled by them. The golden rule underlying good
conflict resolution is:

Attack the problem, not the person.

The best treatise on conflict resolution and anger management in all of literature is found in the Bible: Ephesians chapter 4.

So far we have described *inter-personal* conflict. But sometimes the conflict and pressures come not from within the relationship but from *outside*, such as financial difficulties, the behaviour of friends, colleagues or family, parenting struggles, or illness. These will either draw a couple closer or become a wedge between them. The outcome depends largely on the strength or weakness of their relationship. The problem is never the problem, how they deal with it is the problem. A crisis tests the quality of the intimacy in a marriage.

I, John, was born and brought up in China and understand a little of the language. The Chinese word for *crisis* (wei chi) illustrates a profound psychological truth. It is made up of two separate characters: 'wei' and 'chi'. 'Wei' means *danger* and 'chi' means *opportunity*. So it is with a crisis or a conflict in marriage, it can threaten the relationship or become an opportunity to strengthen it. The choice lies with the couple. Learning to see the potential for intimacy in conflict gives a fresh perspective.

Helen and Tony had been married for twenty-three years and were locked into a pattern of constant conflict. They complained: 'Marriage must have more to offer than this!' For a number of sessions we helped them identify destructive patterns and areas of poor communication in their relationship, but they made slow progress. Then Helen was diagnosed as having breast cancer, and this unexpected threat gave them another focus. They not only determined to face the health challenge together, but were motivated to work constructively on their differences. They lost their competitiveness, finding other-centredness more satisfying.

Mutual Submission

Earlier in this chapter we identified the summary definition of marriage from the Old Testament. The New Testament definition of marriage is even shorter: 'Submit to one another out of reverence for Christ' (Ephesians 5:21). We find that an application of this principle to all aspects of marriage leads to growth in intimacy.

Traditionally it was taught that the wife had to do all the submitting, based on an interpretation of the next verse. But, significantly, the word 'submit' does not occur in verse 22 in the original Greek text. Certainly, it is implied from the verb used in the preceding phrase (a common practice in that language) and therefore is correctly included in our English translations. But the command to submit applies to *both husband and wife*, and the reason given is 'out of reverence for Christ'. This is illustrated in Figure 16.

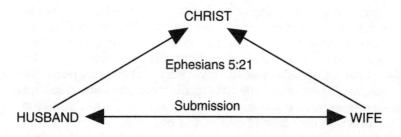

Figure 16. Christian marriage

A Christian husband and wife submit to one another because they acknowledge Christ as the head of their home. Note that verse 23 states that 'the husband is the head of the *wife*', not the home. Headship here does not mean authority. The Greek word *cephale* (head) when used metaphorically most frequently implies 'source' or 'origin'. This is how readers of this first-century document would have understood it. In our Western culture, we equate 'head' with boss, authority or control, and this cultural assumption has led to the misinterpretation of this verse.[23] By contrast, Jesus linked leadership and authority with servanthood.[24] We have a motto in our own relationship: 'I will always be your servant, but you will never be my master.'

Mutual submission takes the sting out of conflict and maintains intimacy. It turns competition into co-operation. Mutual submission provides motivation for other-centredness and a desire to seek each other's welfare at all times. When making big decisions that affect them both, instead of the husband having the casting vote, the outcome is reached as partners discover together what the 'Head' of their marriage wants. This is not just theory, it works.

Sexual Intimacy

Our sexuality was designed by our Creator, not only to attract us to one another, but also to strengthen the intimacy of marriage. Becoming 'one flesh' means far more than physical sex. It implies two people 'weaving together', physically, emotionally and spiritually. A healthy sexual relationship in marriage provides not only on-going pleasure and relaxation, but a means of affirming one another's femaleness and maleness and building self-esteem.

The Clinebells put it this way: 'The raw power of sex is inherent in the fabric of creation – its power is God-given. Regular enjoyment of this powerful source of unity and pleasure is one of the best things about a good marriage.'[25]

But for many couples, sex is disappointing, especially in early marriage. This is because good sex is an art to be learned. Bodies don't make love, people do. Physical love-making can be spoiled by many things: ignorance, negative attitudes, fear of rejection, tension, the pressures of work or child-rearing. The most damaging of all is lack of good communication skills and inability to share feelings, fears and wishes. For those experiencing sexual problems, help is available. There are some excellent books dealing with these issues.[26] Even a few counselling sessions can enable couples to break free from their difficulties and frustrations.

Sex should improve with age, like a good wine. The safety and security of a marriage, based on trust and commitment, provides the best environment for the healthy expression

and development of a sexual relationship. Sexual intercourse can be nourishing, healing and liberating. It is an
important part of the growth of intimacy in marriage. The
very word for sexual intercourse in Scripture (in Hebrew
and Greek) is 'to know'.[27] The Greek word *ginosko* means
'to know thoroughly'; in this context: to know myself and
my partner intimately.

The sexual encounter is perhaps the most sensitive place
where the principle of mutual submission operates. Paul
described it this way: 'The wife's body does not belong
to her alone but also to her husband. In the same way,
the husband's body does not belong to him alone but also
to his wife. Do not deprive each other except by mutual
consent.'[28]

Some men interpret this as the right to unlimited avail-
ability of their partner's body sexually. Actually, the reverse
is true. If the wife's body belongs to her husband, as well
as to her, he has the responsibility to nurture and care for
it and submit to her wishes and needs. This consideration
extends both ways.

Rewarding sexual communication in an on-going relationship depends on good emotional communication. If you
cannot communicate in the living-room you will be unlikely
to do better in the bedroom. Emotional communication is
needed for the full development of a sexual relationship.
No soul-sharing results in superficial sexual intimacy. Thus
satisfying sex helps to build intimacy in a marriage, and
deep intimacy leads to good sex between lovers.

Spiritual Intimacy

St Augustine said: 'Thou hast made us for thyself, and our
hearts are restless until they find their rest in Thee.' This
is as true for couples as it is for individuals. Practical faith
is relational; a living and growing relationship with God.
Two people who share a common faith, jointly draw on
this source of strength as they journey into God together.
'A shared spiritual life strengthens a marriage; conversely, a
good marriage strengthens the spiritual life of the couple.'[29]

The closer partners grow toward God individually, the closer they grow together in their relationship. See Figure 17A.

Figure 17B illustrates the fact that if one partner grows spiritually but the other does not, they will *grow apart* in their own relationship. But in a healthy communicating marriage, partners can help and encourage each other on their spiritual journey. One powerful way to do this is by praying together. Many Christian couples have told us that they do not pray together. They pray separately, but have not discovered the joy and strength of united prayer. Jesus promised his presence when even *two* of his followers meet in his name.[30]

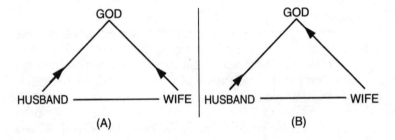

Figure 17. Growing into God

Apart from Jesus' assurance about the effectiveness of this form of praying,[31] praying together provides a window into each other's lives. In this way we can discover each other's concerns, burdens and desires. It is a way of sharing common goals and dreams and gaining perspective on life together. We become more united in purpose and so deepen intimacy.

PLANNED INTIMACY

We have reviewed some dimensions of a growing intimacy in marriage, and there are others. Some aspects of intimacy will appeal more to one couple than to another. Also, as the years go by, the emphasis of their intimacy is likely to change. It is important for each couple to find the right amount, balance and rhythm for their 'dance of intimacy' at their particular stage of life together. Intimacy in a relationship is no accident, it requires work and maintenance. As a simple aid to memory, think in terms of planning times of intimacy on a daily, weekly, monthly and yearly process.

Daily   Never let a day go by without giving each other an *affirmation*: tell her how much you love her; let him know something you value about what he said or did that day. Have a *dialogue* or a sharing of your feelings each day.

Weekly   Set aside time to have at least one special activity just for the two of you each week: go out for coffee or lunch, take a drive or a walk; share communion together at home; spend an evening reading a book or listening to music; write love letters to each other; share the cooking; take time out to enjoy an unhurried, daytime sexual encounter.

Monthly   Arrange a special fun event to enjoy together, such as an afternoon tramp, a swim, a good film or concert, dine out or a romantic night away. It does not have to be expensive to be rewarding. Take turns to plan it as a surprise for your partner.

Yearly   Once a year, perhaps on your wedding anniversary, review your marriage. Write down how you see your relationship developing and in what ways your intimacy is growing. List good things that have happened in your marriage over the past year and areas you would like to improve. Identify some simple goals and objectives for your marriage for the coming year.

Summary

Intimacy in marriage does not come with the wedding ring. It has to be desired and worked for by both partners, who are likely to start out with different expectations as to the amount of intimacy they want. You cannot be intimate with someone you do not know well, and intimacy develops with a deep knowledge of yourself and your partner. The dimensions of intimacy in a marriage are only limited by lack of imagination. True intimacy reflects a balance of all aspects of life together: physical, intellectual, emotional and spiritual.

REFLECTIONS AND EXERCISES

1. LEAVING   Identify the things you brought into your marriage that come from the model you had in your home. Think about your values, beliefs, attitudes and behaviours as it applies to such things as:

   Your communication pattern, ability to share feelings, how you deal with conflict, the way you relate to and discipline your children, attitudes to money, fun, work, sex, faith . . .

   • Discuss whether these are as right for you in your relationship as they might have been for your parents? To what degree have you fully 'left' home?

2. LIVING-TOGETHER-LONELINESS   In your marriage, have there been times of loneliness? Discuss the reasons for this? What could have prevented this loneliness?

3. PERSONALITY TESTS   If you have not done any such tests, it could be helpful to your relationship for you both to do one and find out more about who you are. Many agencies such as business training organisations, universities and psychologists could provide these tests. Read one of the books listed under reference 15, chapter five.

4. LANGUAGES OF LOVE   Refresh your memory of the five most common languages of love. For each of us, one of them will be our primary love language: the way in which we feel and show love best. Other languages may also be familiar and used quite frequently, but one of them usually reaches your heart faster than the others.

   • Arrange these five languages of love in order of significance for you both. Make the assessment on your own, then discuss your conclusions.

5. DAILY DIALOGUE   If you do not already do this,

spend at least fifteen minutes a day in dialogue with your partner, sharing at a feeling level about significant issues. Start each session with an affirmation of each other. Then share something that is really important to you.

- Do this every day for a month, then evaluate how it has affected your relationship.

6. LETTERS   Write a short letter to your husband/wife on one of these topics. Then give it to him/her to read and think about before discussing it in your next dialogue time.

a) The things I find attractive about you.
b) Strengths I/you bring to our marriage.
c) What I enjoy most about our relationship.
d) What could improve our communication.
e) Things I find difficult about our relationship.
f) Things I would like help with from you.
g) My greatest fear.
h) What our sexual relationship means to me.
g) How comfortable I am with our level of intimacy at present.
h) How satisfied I am with the amount we share about spiritual matters.

These by no means cover all the range of possible topics. Keep going with ideas of your own. Try to cover one topic a week.

7. MUTUAL SUBMISSION   Study together Ephesians 5:21–33.

- Is the biblical principle of mutual submission operating in your marriage? What needs to change for this to happen?
- Is the Lord truly the Head of your home? (cp Joshua 24:15)
- How do you make major decisions in your marriage?

• Are you servants to one another? (Mark 10:41–45)

8. SEXUAL INTIMACY   Read through the Song of Solomon together. Use more than one version. (*The Living Bible* gives fresh insights and understandings.) Three excellent studies on this song are listed under reference 32.

TEN

INTIMACY WITH GOD

Come near to God and he will come near to you.
James, c. AD 50[1]

Having looked at aspects of human intimacy, we turn now to the vital theme of intimacy with God. The two are related. Experiencing human intimacy opens us to intimacy with God, and intimacy with him transforms human closeness. 'We cannot live in intimate communion with Jesus without being sent out to our brothers and sisters who belong to the same humanity that Jesus accepted as his own.'[2]

But how can finite beings experience intimacy with the Infinite? The exciting truth is that *even desiring* this encounter is evidence of God seeking us. Following those stirrings, doing our part to respond and 'come near', is to move actively towards God. We discover then that God welcomes us to intimacy with himself. Many books have been written on this topic by people more experienced than ourselves. However, in this final chapter, we explore how intimacy with God is similar to human intimacy described earlier in this book, and follow the same pattern using as subheadings the chapter titles.

LONELINESS

A common response to loneliness is to fill our emptiness with other things: people, activities, distractions and pursuits of one kind and another. Even substance abuse is essentially a spiritual quest. Out of this longing there comes to most of us, at some time, a desire for reality and meaning. We are not satisfied. God uses our existential loneliness to draw us to himself. 'To many, the spiritual desert is a place of "*katharsis*", of stripping and nakedness, of man's terrible aloneness and God's mysterious revealing.'[3]

Experiencing relational loneliness, failed friendships, and lack of intimacy, makes us aware of our deep inner loneliness. If we are prepared to listen, we will discover that God is there for us in these situations. He is 'more intimate to us than we are to ourselves'.[4] Loneliness may lead to our initial encounter with God, and can be an on-going reminder of our need of him.

We come to God mostly in times of need, when we realise our inadequacies, lack of fulfilment, or that we are less than whole. But God is not there just to fill our deficiencies. He wants to be invited into *every part* of our lives: spirit, soul and body. 'Love the Lord your God with all your heart and with all your soul and with all your strength and with all your mind.'[5]

FRIENDSHIP

Intimacy with God implies friendship. Abraham and Moses were the only ones in Old Testament times to be called 'friends of God'.[6] When Jesus came to reveal God to ordinary men and women, he invited them to know and experience God personally. He calls his followers 'my friends'.[7] Throughout the biography of Jesus, we see him reaching out in friendship, love and compassion. He met people at their point of need and touched the deep centre of their longing, offering hope, healing and wholeness through a relationship with himself. Jesus did not force himself on people, he gave them the choice to follow him or not.[8] He also looks for a chosen love response from us. Refusing his friendship is to miss out on that for which we were created.

There are many ways in which friendship with God can

be expressed. As a woman, I (Agnes) often identify with the story of Martha and Mary and their friendship with Jesus. I have a real empathy for Martha in her busyness and envy Mary's ability to focus on Jesus, despite distractions. Martha showed her friendship in service and Mary in just being with her Friend.[9] Both are appropriate responses, but not one to the exclusion of the other. God invites us all to the wonder of friendship with himself. 'Friendship with God is reserved for those who reverence him.'[10]

INTIMACY

Intimacy with God presumes a close relationship. In families we learn about relationships, first with mother, then father, often with sisters and brothers. Later we relate to friends, companions, work mates. We may experience the love relationship of a lifetime partnership. In coming to God, some of these relationship experiences can help us know God as Father and Mother and Jesus as our brother, friend and companion. If relationships in our families and with friends have only been superficial, we are likely to expect that our relationship with God will be the same. But if we have experienced human intimacy, this will prepare us for intimacy with God.

We sometimes presume that knowing about God equals knowing him personally; that studying the Bible will result in closeness to him. This becomes true only if we give time to developing intimacy with God. Jesus said to the Jews: 'You diligently study the Scriptures because you think that by them you possess eternal life. [They] testify about me, yet you refuse to come to me to have life.'[11] Intimacy with God is his present to us. It is possible to focus on the wrapping paper and ignore the gift inside.

The image of *lover* depicts true intimacy. This metaphor is used in Scripture to describe God's relationship with us.[12] The theme of God's love is like a thread woven through the Bible. We frequently read of his 'everlasting love', 'steadfast love', 'unfailing love', 'boundless love', 'loving-kindness enduring for ever'. He loved his people, the Israelites, just because he chose to, not because they deserved it.[13] The Old Testament prophets wrote passionately about the God who longed for his people to draw near to him. The Psalms are songs about the love and mercy of God.

The central book in the Bible is the Song of Songs, an intimate love poem about two lovers. Both the bride and the bridegroom express their love equally. This is a picture of God's love for us, and ours for him. The powerful emotions expressed here between two human lovers typifies our relationship with the Heavenly Lover. 'I belong to my lover, and his desire is for me.'[14] This can be the experience of every human being who seeks intimacy with God.

God is portrayed in Scripture as the God who *reveals* himself. Jesus came to earth as a human being to reveal God's character and the extent of his love for us. He is described as 'the Word', the very expression of God.[15] This was the only way that we could know what God was like. Jesus has also made intimacy with God possible. This theme is the thesis of the book of Hebrews.

As was pointed out in chapters three and seven, we can only love and feel close to someone we know. Intimacy depends on two people revealing themselves to each other. Our intimacy with God develops as we take time to discover the many ways he reveals himself to us. We must also become vulnerable to God, and share our feelings with him. This is not because God does not already know all about us. He does. Rather, it is because the Lover desires this self-revelation from the beloved. This is the essence of a love relationship. How often our prayers come more from the head than the heart, as we share our thoughts but not our feelings. The Psalms are a wonderful model of how to share feelings, both 'positive' and 'negative', with God.[16]

HISTORY

Chapter four describes some historical and sociological trends in human intimacy. Over the centuries, many great

women and men have recorded their experience of intimacy
with God. Paul set the pattern: 'I consider everything a
loss compared to the surpassing greatness of *knowing*
Christ Jesus my Lord.' He encouraged others to follow
his example.[17]

Some, like the early Desert Fathers and Mothers of the
fourth and fifth centuries escaped to the desert, avoiding
the hurly-burly of life to experience God more deeply.
Others followed them there to learn from them, and then
returned to normal life enriched by the experience. This
desire to set one's life apart to experience God resulted in the
establishment of Religious Orders. Today we benefit from
the writings of some of these great men and women of God.
But life in a monastery does not avoid distractions. Brother
Lawrence, as he served his fellow monks, demonstrated that
intimacy with God took practice. He wrote: 'The time of
busyness does not differ with me from the time of prayer;
and in the noise and clatter of my kitchen, while several
persons are at the same time calling for different things,
I possess God in as great tranquillity as if I were on my
knees.'[18]

We owe much of our spiritual heritage to three devout
people who lived in the sixteenth century. Ignatius of
Loyola described a form of prayer in his 'Spiritual Exercises'. This is a way of discovering Jesus through meditation
on Scripture passages. We both find this a helpful practice
to follow. John of the Cross discovered that for him, God
was found in 'the dark night of the soul', and that this
comes to many who give themselves seriously to a life
of prayer.[19] Teresa of Avila described the journey of faith
in her 'interior castle' image.[20] To attain full union with
Christ in the inner sanctuary, she describes a progression
through various 'rooms' or stages.

Contemporary authors, such as A.W. Tozer, C.S. Lewis,
Catherine Marshall and Richard Foster inspire and challenge us to experience intimacy with God. Examples of a
more contemplative approach are the writings of Thomas
Merton, Henri Nouwen and Evelyn Underhill. These and

many others have set the pace for us to follow in developing our own experience of intimacy with God. Currently, the *Exploring Prayer Series*, edited by Joyce Huggett, deals with aspects of prayer to suit modern but earnest followers of Jesus, bringing them to intimacy and a soul relationship with him. (See Bibliography.)

For each of us, intimacy with God is individual and unique. As we spend time with our Heavenly Lover, we hear him say: 'I love no one more than I love you, but I don't love you more than anyone else.'[21] Accepting, believing and feeling this helps us on our journey to true intimacy with God.

INTIMACY WITH SELF

Understanding, knowing and valuing oneself can move in parallel with a growing intimacy with God. As already quoted from Psalm 139, David asks God to search and know his heart. This is a request to know himself, the person God created him to be, his inner longings, weaknesses and failings. A New Testament example of this is Peter. As he came to know Jesus, so he discovered things about himself.[22] As we too develop insights about ourselves and share these in prayer, so we come to appreciate our God-image better, as males or females.

This helps to facilitate our knowledge of who God is and deepen our relationship with him. In Jesus, God experienced what it was like to be human, as well as providing a way for us to know him. As perfect man, Jesus made the bridge between us and a holy God, so that even in our imperfection we can relate to him.

Because God is love, the relationship grows into his love, and our response is to become more loving. This embraces loving God, others and ourselves. His grace, his love-gift to us, makes this possible. Sharing our feelings with God in prayer maintains intimacy with him. God in turn comes to us in a myriad ways, especially as we open every aspect of our lives to him. Thomas Merton wrote:

A genuine discovery of Christ within our own being is not possible until we have courageously faced the truth about who we are, accepting all our limitations, and being free to accept others as they are, with all their limitations. Union is effected by God himself, and remains always a mystery.[23]

BLOCKS TO INTIMACY

The blocks that keep us from intimacy with God are similar to those which prevent human intimacy. However, in relating to God we move into another dimension. We are developing a relationship with the transcendent God, Creator and Saviour. He desires this more than we do, so the blocks are of our making. We will list a few of them, but not an exhaustive list, as each person in their uniqueness has their own.

- *Doubt* is a common block, thinking that God is not there.
- *Desire* for God may be missing, as we fill our emptiness with many other things.
- *Distorted thinking* about God, arising from our child-hood perceptions or later experiences and fears.
- *Distancing* ourselves by wanting our own way. As someone has said: 'If you don't feel close to God, guess who moved?'
- *Denying* our own value to God: 'I'm not worth loving.'

As we recognise our blocks and deal with them in appropriate ways, they can become stepping-stones to greater intimacy. For example, looking at doubt for what it really is, and turning it into faith as I believe God's Word, even though I do not feel it. This takes perseverance on my part, and an openness to God's Spirit. Sometimes the block is our distorted thinking, creating God in our image. We may see him as a policeman, a 'sugar-daddy', a benign grandfather who is out of touch, a perfectionist, a managing director, and many other such distortions.[24]

Spiritual growth comes as we deal with blocks. This process takes time, honesty and a willingness to let go of them. Just as a child clings to familiar toys, so we are reluctant to let go of things we have held on to and believed in, even when they are shown to be wrong. Some blocks may reappear after we think we have dealt with them. Our humanness is a barrier, but God meets us in our limitations. 'The Spirit helps us in our weakness.'[25]

KEYS TO INTIMACY

Keys unlock doors, suitcases and hidden areas. To experience intimacy with Almighty God we also need keys, and to discover our own personal ones. Someone else's key may help me, but I require my own for my unique relationship with God. In a sense we need a series of keys, as often one room leads to another in our journey into God, as already described. We will identify a few of the keys available.

Relational Keys

In chapter seven we describe some keys for human intimacy, and these also apply to our relationship with God.

Mutual Desire
This is essential for intimacy between two people. There is no doubt about God's desire for fellowship with us, and we are invited to intimacy with him. 'Come near to God and he will come near to you.'[26] We can be as close to God as we want to be.

Autonomy
Human relationships function best when there is both autonomy and intimacy, as each person offers the other freedom and choice. Relationships are stifled if one person swamps the other. God offers us the dignity of choosing to be near to him, because he wants our love to be freely given. He does not force himself on us, but will transform us with his life to the degree that we desire this.

Other-Centredness
This is the principle ingredient of human intimacy. God's
love is defined by its unconditional giving nature: 'God so
loved that he gave . . .'[27] Our response must be the same:
a focus on God and freely giving our love and ourselves
to him.

Devotional Keys

Scripture
Earlier we described the Bible as 'God's love letter to us.'
There is no better way to discover God than to know what
he is saying to us in Scripture. As we read his Word
thoughtfully and prayerfully, so the Holy Spirit speaks
these truths into our hearts.

Meditation
The word meditation comes from the same Latin root as
the word 'medicine'. Neither medicine nor Scripture will
do us good unless we inwardly absorb and digest it.
Biblical meditation is the devotional practice of pondering
on, feeding on and delighting in a portion of Scripture.[28]
We can also meditate on God's works in nature.[29] In a
'contemplative walk', we can use all our senses to absorb
something of what he is telling us of himself through
creation.

In meditation 'the Bible ceases to be a quotation diction-
ary, and becomes instead wonderful words of life that lead
us to *the* Word of Life'.[30] It has often been compared to
rumination, the way a cow chews its cud over and over
again. Another beautiful metaphor is that of conception. In
motherhood, the new life within is nurtured, fed, protected,
fostered and allowed to grow. The mother is aware of
movement within and changes taking place in her body
as a result of the new life. So in meditation 'we can find
a new purpose in being, for we carry the word within'.[31]
Eventually it comes to birth and fulfils its purpose.

Judeo-Christian meditation differs significantly from

Eastern meditation and Transcendental Meditation. The goal of Eastern meditation is to free the mind of all thought and imagery in order to attain 'bliss consciousness' or 'pure being'. The goal of Christian meditation is to fill the mind with truth, love and beauty and to know God better. The basis of Eastern meditation is that the answer to life's quest is *in me*. The basis of Christian meditation is that the answer to life's quest is *in God*.[32]

Prayer
Listening to God and responding to him in prayer helps that intimate relationship to grow. We sometimes limit prayer to a 'shopping list' of needs. The acronym ACTS summarises other aspects of prayer: Adoration, Confession, Thanksgiving and Supplication. Adoration means focussing on God himself and responding with worship from our total being. It means moving from our one-sided conversations as we learn to listen to God, to hearing his voice in the stillness. A helpful book on this process is *Listening to God*, by Joyce Huggett.[33]

Contemplation
In contemplation we move from 'head' prayer to 'heart' prayer. It has been called 'loving attentiveness to God', or 'the prayer of empty hands'. It is not saying, asking or doing – just *being* in God's presence. 'Be still and know that I am God.'[34] The essence of contemplative prayer is silence, solitude and simplicity. Jim Borst states: 'Contemplation is prayer of heart and will which reaches out to God's presence. The lips and mind both come to rest. There is a simple gazing at the Lord while the heart reaches out in wordless prayer, and the will seeks to be one with his.'[35]

Journalling
This process was described in chapter five as a helpful way to grow in understanding ourselves. It can also assist our personal journey with God and to God. 'For the Christian,

the journal's main function is to record the unfolding relationship between our Creator and ourselves. Because God is
so important, his dealings with us are worth recording.'[36]

Communion
At the Lord's table, we enjoy his presence in fellowship
with others. Here we can find intimacy with the suffering
Christ, appreciating and participating in his death and
resurrection. As we take the bread and wine, we feed
on him in our hearts, and in this mystery we experience
intimacy with the Lord.

Spiritual Direction
This process provides help on the journey towards know-
ing and experiencing God through a guide and mentor.
(See chapter five.) Spiritual direction in the prayer life of
individuals helps them discern the movements of the Holy
Spirit within.

Books
Many books are available that can give us a greater under-
standing and meet a growing desire in our hearts to know
God better. We refer to a number of them in this chapter.

SINGLENESS AND INTIMACY WITH GOD

We both look back to days before marriage and remember
how we planned times of quiet to read and pray, whenever
it suited us and for as long as we liked. This was not so easy
after we married, especially with family responsibilities.
Paul stated that an advantage of the single life was the
opportunity for 'undivided devotion to the Lord', whereas
a married person's 'interests are divided'.[37]

Intimacy with God develops best in solitude and silence,
two things that are usually missing from marriage and
family life! This is one of the attractions which draws people
into religious communities. We also have friends in secular
occupations who have chosen singleness, primarily for the

same reason. They are spiritually rich and fulfilled people. We all have equal potential for developing intimacy with God, but single people have a greater freedom to pursue this goal.

MARRIAGE AND INTIMACY WITH GOD

It is easier for us to write from experience on this topic. We have found that the growing intimacy of our own relationship has given us greater insights into the relationship God seeks with us. Marriage models the relationship between Christ and the Church, which is called his bride.[38] This is a frequent metaphor in Scripture.[39] The Song of Solomon depicts poetically the love relationship between a man and a woman, but is also an allegory of the love that is possible between God and us.

While marriage partners can distract each other from intimacy with God, they can also encourage one another in this purpose. We commented in chapter nine on the value of praying together. We can also challenge and stimulate one another in spiritual growth. In the demands of family life we can provide opportunity for each other to have space and quiet by taking over full family responsibility for periods of time. When one partner finds the spiritual journey hard, the other can provide encouragement.

At the same time, each partner is responsible for his or her own intimacy with God. We cannot produce spiritual maturity in our partner, but can give each other space to grow towards God in the particular way God has for them. An intimate relationship between a man and a woman should promote and not hinder each other's intimacy with God. Temple Gairdner wrote this poem just before his marriage.[40]

That I may come near to her,
    draw me nearer to Thee than to her.
That I may know her,
    make me to know Thee more than her.

That I may love her with the perfect love
    of a perfectly whole heart,
      cause me to love Thee more than her, and most of
        all
That nothing may be between me and her,
    be Thou between us every moment.
That we may be constantly together,
    draw us unto separate loneliness with Thyself.
And when we meet breast to breast, O God,
    let it be upon Thine own.

Summary

There is a strong parallel between the principles of human intimacy and our intimacy with God. These have been built into us because we are made in God's image as relational beings. Jesus modelled perfect human intimacy in his relationships with people and with God. He also made intimacy with God possible for us. We can be as near to God as we desire to be, and God longs for this closeness more than we do.

REFLECTIONS AND EXERCISES

1. FRIENDSHIP   To what degree do you see God, or Jesus, as your friend. From your experience of human relationships, what aspects of friendship would you want to develop with God? For example: friends like to spend time together, discover each other's thoughts, express their feelings for one another, share their vision, hopes and fears.

   • Write a letter to your 'Divine Friend', incorporating some of these things.

2. Use the words of Psalm 18:1 to start expressing your love for God – 'Lord, how I love you! For you have done such tremendous things for me' (TLB). Tell him all the reasons why you love him. It may help to write them in your journal.

3. IGNATIAN STYLE PRAYER
   a) Start by asking for God's grace, guidance and insight.
   b) Read a Gospel narrative, e.g.
        John 21:1–17; Luke 7:36–50;
        Luke 24:13–32.
   c) Imagine the scene in detail, using your five senses. What can you see, hear, touch, smell, taste?
   d) Be one of the characters. What would you say to others present, and what might they say to you? Notice your reactions, responses and resistances.
   e) Savour and stay with the feelings of being with Jesus. Keep turning your attention to him. Finally, thank him for your intimate time together and for his promise to be always with you.

4 MEDITATION   Spend some time meditating on the words of Jesus:

   'Here I am! I stand at the door and knock. If anyone hears my voice and opens the door, I will come

in and eat with him/her, and she/he with me'
(Revelation 3:20).

Be aware of Jesus waiting, knocking and asking to come
in. How long has it been since you invited him in for a
meal – a sharing time together? He desires this as much
as you need it.

Jesus said: 'I will eat *with him.*' He wants to eat of *your
bread.* What have you to offer him? He also said: 'and he
will eat *with me.*' What food is he offering you today?
What do you need from him?

5 HOLIDAY WITH GOD   Spend a day alone at a beach,
in the country or bush. Have no other agenda but to
enjoy his company, read from nature, 'his other book'.
Listen to him and talk with him.

- A more formal way to do this is to spend a day or
  more at a retreat centre. It could be a guided retreat
  or a silent one. Spending some days in a silent retreat
  can be a life-changing experience.

CONCLUSION

We have been created with a longing for intimacy, but we are not born with the skills to make it happen. There are three main aspects to intimacy. (See Figure 18.) The journey begins as we discover an intimacy with ourselves. Only then are we ready to experience intimacy with others. We are also designed for intimacy with God, and our human existence is incomplete without this. The keys to human intimacy and intimacy with God are similar.

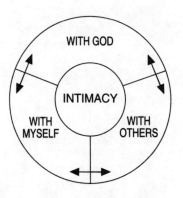

Figure 18: A model of the dimensions of intimacy

CREATED FOR INTIMACY

Our wholeness as people is found as we grow in these three areas of intimacy. Each dimension affects the other two, and we are incomplete when one of them is missing or under-developed. Our prayer is that this book may help you on your journey to knowing yourself and experiencing intimacy with others and with God.

APPENDIX ONE
NOTES AND REFERENCES

INTRODUCTION

1) John 17:3; Ephesians 1:17; Philippians 3:8,10.
2) J. and A. Sturt, *Created for Love* (Eagle, Guildford, 1994).
3) Lawrence Osborne, *Paper Pilgrimage* (London, Daybreak, 1990) pp 2–3.

CHAPTER ONE

1) Psalm 102:7 (The Living Bible).
2) L. Peplau and D. Perlman (Editors) *Loneliness: A Sourcebook of Current Theory, and Therapy* (New York, John Wiley & Sons, 1982). A valuable overview of research and literature on loneliness.
3) Ibid, p 332.
4) Daniel Defoe, *Robinson Crusoe* (New York, Signet, 1960).
5) Isaiah 5:8.
6) James J. Lynch, *The Broken Heart: The Medical Consequences of Loneliness* (New York, Basic Books, 1977).
7) James J. Lynch, *The Language of The Heart* (New York, Basic Books, 1985) p 69.
8) G.M. Maxwell and B. Coeberg 'Patterns of Loneliness in a New Zealand Population', *Community Mental Health in New Zealand*, Vol 2, No. 2, 1986, pp 48–61.
9) Health Statistical Services, Department of Health, Wellington, 1990 The age specific suicide rate for males in the age group rose steadily over the decade to 40 per 100,000, double that of 1980.
10) Genesis 1:31.
11) Genesis 1:26.
12) Joyce Huggett, *Just Good Friends* (Leicester, UK, Inter-Varsity Press, 1985) p 16.
13) 1 Corinthians 10:11. See also 2 Peter 2:6.

14) Dan Kiley, *Living Together, Feeling Alone: Healing Your Inner Loneliness* (New York, Prentice Hall, 1989).

15) Gerson, C and Perlman, D, 'Loneliness and Expressive Communication', *Journal of Abnormal Psychology*, 1979, vol 88, No. 3, pp 258–261.

16) 1 Corinthians 2:11 (The Living Bible).

17) St Augustine of Hippo, *Confessions*: Book 1, chapter 1.

18) Jeremiah 2:13.

19) R. Paloutzain and C. Craig, in *Loneliness: A Sourcebook of Current Theory, Research and Therapy* (New York, John Wiley & Sons, 1982) chapter 14, p 234.

20) Revelation 3:20.

21) Hebrews 13:5b.

22) John 7:5.

23) John 6:66.

24) Matthew 26:56; Mark 14:50.

25) Matthew 27:46. When separated from his Father, Jesus addressed him as 'God' (Hebrew: *El*) not, Abba, his usual term. Compare Luke 23:46, after the period of separation.

26) Hebrews 4:15.

27) Ecclesiastes 1:14,17; 2:11,17,26; 4:4,6.

28) Henri J.M. Nouwen, *Out of Solitude* (Indiana, Notre Dame, Ave Maria Press, 1990) p 26.

29) A.G. Weiss, 'Privacy and Intimacy', *Journal of Humanistic Psychology*, 27(1) December, 1987, p 122.

30) Henri J.M. Nouwen, *The Way of the Heart* (London, Daybreak, second edition, 1989) p 26.

31) Stephanie Dowrick, *Intimacy and Solitude – Changing Your Life* (Auckland, Reed Publishing, New Zealand, Ltd, 1991).

32) Thomas Merton, *The Silent Life* (New York, Farrar, Strauss & Giroux, 1957) p 38.

33) 1 Kings 18 and 19.

34) Isaiah 30:15.

35) Examples: after a busy day (Mark 1:35); before an important decision (Luke 6:12). Luke records 8 occasions where Jesus withdrew for quietness and prayer.

36) Carl Jung, 1875–1961, Swiss psychiatrist, contributed greatly to understanding personality and dream analysis.

37) Deuteronomy 8:2.

38) This experience is described in Psalm 84:5–7.

39) Joyce Huggett, op cit, p 140.

40) Paula Ripple, *Walking With Loneliness* (Indiana, Notre Dame, Ave Maria Press, 1982) p 15.

CHAPTER TWO

1) Ben Sira, *The Apocrypha*, Ecclesiasticus 6:16.
2) Aristotle, *Nicomachean Ethics*, Book viii, Sec 1.
3) Robert Brain, *Friends and Lovers* (London, Granada Publishing, 1976).
4) Jocelyn Grantham, Auckland, New Zealand, 1995.
5) J. Bowlby, *Attachment and Loss* (London, Hogarth Press, 1969–82).
6) Pythagoras, Diogenes Laertius, *Pythagoras*, Sec 10.
7) Deuteronomy 13:6 (KJV). 'Thy friend which is as thine own soul.'
8) Dale Carnegie, *How to Win Friends and Influence People – Revised Edition* (New York, Simon and Schuster, 1981).
9) Proverbs 17:17.
10) C.S. Lewis, *The Four Loves* (London, Collins, 1960).
11) Robert Brain, ibid, p 19.
12) John Powell and Loretta Brady, *Will the Real Me Please Stand Up* (Valencia, CA, Tabor Publishing, 1985) p 102.
13) Romans 15:7.
14) R.W. Emerson, *Essays, First Series: Friendship* (1841).
15) J. and A. Sturt, *Created for Love* (Guildford, Eagle, 1994) p 115 ff. Explores the relationship of low self-esteem to selfishness.
16) John 15:13.
17) Philippians 2:4. (Contrast with verse 21.)
18) Samuel Butler, 1612–1680, British poet, satirist, author of the poem *Hudibras*.
19) Proverbs 19:4, 6,7.
20) K. & L. Kristen, *Marriage and The Family* (New York, Harper and Row, 1988) p 536.
21) 1 Corinthians 13:7 (The Living Bible). Him/her inserts are ours.
22) Proverbs 27:17 (Good News Bible).
23) Sir Francis Bacon, *Essays: Of Friendship* (1612).
24) Ecclesiastes 4:8–12 (The Living Bible). Emphasis ours.
25) Proverbs 13:17 (The Living Bible).
26) James 1:19.
27) Anne Long, *Listening* (London, Daybreak, 1990) p 57.
28) John Powell, ibid, p 109.
29) Robert Bolton, *People Skills* (New Jersey, Prentice-Hall, 1979) p 50.
30) See Proverbs 14:10; 1 Corinthians 2:11, especially in The Living Bible.

CHAPTER THREE

1) Song of Solomon 5:16, the Shulamite (bride) speaking.
2) Carl Jung first used *persona* (Latin for 'mask', especially when worn by an actor) to refer to 'image' or 'personage'.
3) This concept of personal and combined space is drawn from *The Art of Intimacy* by Thomas and Patrick Malone (New York, Simon and Schuster, 1987) chapter 1.
4) The 'castle' metaphor is elaborated in our book *Created for Love* (Guildford, Eagle, 1994) chapter 10.
5) Erik Erickson, *Insight and Responsibility* (New York, Norton, 1964) p 128.
6) S. Dowrick, *Intimacy and Solitude* (Auckland, Reed Publishing, New Zealand, Ltd., 1991) p 196.
7) H. I. Reis, 'The role of intimacy in interpersonal relations', *Journal of Social and Clinical Psychology*, 1990, 9(1), p 16.
8) 1 Samuel 18:1.
9) John 13:23; 19:26; 20:2; 21:7, 20.
10) John 13:1, 34; 21:15–17.
11) *The Iliad* and *The Odessy* by Homer, blind poet of Greece (c. 900 BC) Lengthy poems contain many stories of Greek gods and human heroes.
12) Robert Brain, *Friends and Lovers* (London, Hart-Davis, MacGibbon, 1976) p 30.
13) Ibid p 38ff.
14) Explored by Stuart Miller in *Men and Friendship* (San Leandro, CA, Gateway Books, 1983).
15) Roy McCloughry, *Men and Masculinity* (London, Hodder and Stoughton, 1992) p 118.
16) Lionel Tiger, *Men in Groups* (London, Nelson, 1969) p 44.
17) Attributed to the Duke of Wellington (who defeated Napoleon at Waterloo in 1815) while watching sport at Eton.
18) Ronald Levant: *Time Magazine*, January 20, 1992, p 44.
19) C. Rubenstein, and P. Shaver, *In Search Of Intimacy* (New York, Delacorte Press, 1982) p 25.
20) Ruth 1:16,17 (TLB). Ruth was a Moabite and Naomi an Israelite, about 1300 BC.
21) Deborah Tannen, *You Just Don't Understand* (Australia, Random House, 1990).
22) Title of a book by John Gray (New York, Harper-Collins, 1992) which explores this issue.

CHAPTER FOUR

1) William Shakespeare, *Henry IV, Part 2*, Act 3, Sc 21 (1597).
2) Plato, 427–347 BC, the second of the great trio of ancient Greek philosophers, Socrates, Plato and Aristotle.
3) Genesis 2:7 (KJV).
4) Leon Battista Alberti (1404–1472), Italian Humanist, principal initiator of Renaissance art theory.
5) René Descartes (1596–1650), French mathematician, lawyer, philosopher and writer.
6) T.S. Ashton, *The Industrial Revolution 1760–1830* (London, Oxford University Press, 1961) p 143.
7) *Time*, Weekly Newsmagazine, January 11, 1993.
8) T.S. Ashton, op cit, p 128.
9) New Zealand Official Yearbook, 1990 and 1995.
10) Henri Nouwen, *With Open Hands* (Indiana, Ave Maria Press, 1995) p 21
11) Roy McCloughry, *Men and Masculinity* (London, Hodder and Stoughton, 1992) p 189.
12) New Zealand Official Yearbook, 1995.
13) Ecclesiastes 4:4.
14) Genesis 12:10–20.
15) Genesis 20:1–18.
16) Genesis 26:7–11.
17) 1 Peter 3:6 (AV).
18) Matthew 19:3.
19) Deuteronomy 24:1–4; Matthew 19:7,8.
20) Adin Steinssaltz, *The Essential Talmud* (USA, Bantam Books Ltd, 1976) p 137.
21) Ibid, p 128. Comment by R. Eliazar.
22) Qur'an, Sura iv: 34.
23) Qur'an, iv: 3.
24) Jean Sasson, *Princess* (London, Bantam Books, 1993) p 21.
25) Matthew 19:10.
26) John 4:3–30.
27) Luke 7:37–50; John 8:1–11.
28) Matt 26:13.
29) John 19:25–27.
30) John 20:17.
31) Ephesians 5:25,28.
32) Ephesians 5:21. Note: the word 'submit' does not occur in v 22 in

the original Greek. It is implied from v 21, where both husband and wife are instructed to submit mutually.

33) Augustine, 430–534 AD, *De Genesi ad Litteram*, VII, 3.

34) Tertullian, 160–220 AD, *On The Apparel of Women* Book 1, Ch. 1.

35) Letha Scanzoni, *Why Wait* (Grand Rapids, Baker Book House, 1975) p 27. She outlines the negative attitudes of the early church to women, marriage and sex.

36) Augustine, *On The Holy Trinity*, Select Library of the Nicene and Post-Nicene Fathers, Vol III (Grand Rapids, Eerdmans, 1956) p 159.

37) Quoted by M. Potter in 'Gender Equality and Gender Hierarchy in Calvin's Theology', *Signs: Journal of Women in Culture and Society*, Vol II, no. 4.

38) *Luther's Works*, vol 54, *Tabletalk* (Fortress Press, 1967) p 8.

39) Genesis 1:27,28.

40) Mary Stewart Van Lewen et al, *After Eden: Facing the Challenge of Gender Reconciliation* (Grand Rapids, Eerdmans, 1993) p 7.

41) Ann Brown, *Apology to Women: Christian Images of the Female Sex* (Leicester, Inter-Varsity Press, 1991) p 11. Excellent description of traditional Christian attitudes to women.

42) Genesis 3:16.

43) Genesis 4:7.

44) Germaine Greer, *The Female Eunuch* (London, MacGibbon and Key, 1970).

45) Some useful additional titles:
    Elaine Storkey, *What's Right with Feminism?* (London, SPCK/*Third Way*, 1985).
    Mary Evans, *Women and the Bible* (Exeter, Paternoster Press, 1983).
    Letha Scanzoni & Nancy Hardesty, *All We're Meant To Be* (Waco, Word, 1974).

46) Galatians 3:28.

47) John 8:32–36.

48) Harry Tegnaeus, *Blood-brothers* (Stockholm, 1952).

49) Robert Brain, *Friends and Lovers* (London, Hart-Davis, MacGibbon, 1976) p 91. Source of some anthropological information cited here.

50) J.W. Mintz, and E.R. Wolf, *An Analysis of Ritual Co-godparenthood* (1950).

CHAPTER FIVE

1) Socrates was an Athenian philosopher. He wrote no books, but his teaching profoundly affected Greek thought, influencing Plato and

Aristotle. These three laid the philosophical foundation of Greek, and subsequently Western culture.

2) 2 Corinthians 13:5 (KJV).

3) Romans 12:3 (J.B. Phillips).

4) Paul Tournier, *The Meaning of Persons* (London, SCM Press, 1957).

5) John 16:13; 8:32.

6) John 3:34 (TLB); see also Psalm 111:10; Proverbs 1:7; 9:10; 14:27; 15:33; Isaiah 33:6.

7) For a psychological and biblical understanding of the 'self', see *Me, Myself, and I* by Archibald Hart (Guildford, Highland, 1992).

8) Psalm 139:1 and 23.

9) Genesis 1:27.

10) Morton and Barbara Kelsey, *Sacrament of Sexuality: The Spirituality and Psychology of Sex* (New York, Amity House Ltd, 1986).

11) Psalm 139:16; Jeremiah 1:5; Luke 1:35; Galatians 1:15.

12) J. Reisman, and E. Eichel, *Kinsey, Sex and Fraud* (Lafayette, Louisiana, Lochinvar-Huntington House, 1990). The previously often-quoted figure of 10% of the population being homosexual has been proved inaccurate.

13) Elizabeth Moberly, *Homosexuality, A New Christian Ethic* (Trowbridge, Redwood Burn Ltd, 1983).

14) A beautiful example of this is recorded in John 4.

15) Isobel Myers: *Gifts Differing* (Oxford, Oxford Psychological Press, 1990). The title is taken from Romans 12:6 (KJV). Two useful books in understanding the MBTI theory are:
a) *Knowing Me, Knowing You* by Malcolm Goldsmith and Martin Wharton (London, SPCK, 1993). These two Christian ministers explore the relationship between type and spirituality.
b) *Please Understand Me* by David Keirsey and Marilyn Bates (Del Mar, California, Prometheus Nemesis Books, 1984).

16) Carl Jung, *Psychological Types* (New York, Harcourt Brace, 1923).

17) A helpful book on this topic is *Prayer and Temperament: Different Prayer Forms for Different Personality Types* by Chester Michael and Marie Norrisey (Charlottesville, Open Door, 1991).

18) R.M. Taylor, and W.L. Morrison, *Taylor-Johnson Temperament Analysis, Manual and Handbook* (Los Angeles, Psychological Publications, 1984).

19) The T-JTA test was designed in North America. Its application to non-Western cultures has not been established.

20) Galatians 5:22,23. M.C. Porter has compared the nine fruits of the Spirit to the nine traits tested by T-JTA.

21) A common NT theme. See Ephesians 4:13; 2 Corinthians 3:18; James 1:4.

22) John Powell, *The Christian Vision, The Truth that Sets Us Free* (Allen, Texas, Argus Communications, 1984).

23) There are over 700 references to the 'heart' in Scripture. Examples: Psalm 14:1; 15:2; 139:23; Proverbs 3:5; Matthew 5:8; Romans 10:9.

24) The two main ways in which the human heart can be spiritually renewed: the work of God's Spirit (Ezekiel 36:26) and the influence of the Word of God (Hebrews 4:12).

25) J. and A. Sturt, *Created for Love* (Guildford, Eagle, 1994) chapter 4.

26) From Paul Tournier, *The Meaning of Persons*, see note 4 above.

27) Leviticus 19:18; Matthew 22:39; Mark 12:31; Romans 13:9; Galatians 5:14; Ephesians 5:28,33; James 2:8.

28) J. and A. Sturt, op cit, chapter 10.

29) Matthew 13:12.

30) 'Journal' comes from French 'le jour' (the day). Diary and journal are both derived from Latin *diurnalis* (daily). 'Journey' is from the same root.

31) Luci Shaw, *Life Path: Personal and Spiritual Growth Through Journal Writing* (Portland, Multnomah, 1991)

32) From Philippians 4:8 (*The Message*).

33) Herman Riffel: *Your Dreams: God's Neglected Gift* (Lincoln, Virginia, Chosen Books, 1981) p 25.

34) Other useful books on dreams:
C.G. Jung, *Memories, Dreams, Reflections*, edited by Aniela Jaffe (New York, Harcourt, Brace & Co, 1933).
Morton Kelsey, *Dreams: A Way to Listen to God* (New York, Paulist Press, 1982).
Russ Parker, *Healing Dreams* (London, SPCK, 1988).
Savary, Berne and Williams, *Dreams and Spiritual Growth: A Christian Approach to Dreamwork* (New Jersey, Paulist Press, 1984).

35) Dag Hammerskjold, 1905–1961, second Secretary General of the United Nations.

36) Barry and Connolly, *The Practice of Spiritual Direction* (New York, The Seabury Press, 1983) p 8.

37) This section is adapted from the appendix on Growth Groups, in *Created for Love*, op cit.

38) Howard Clinebell, *Growth Groups* (Nashville, Abingdon, 1977) p 2. He describes using growth groups in a variety of situations: for singles, marrieds, families and churches.

39) 1 Corinthians 12:12–31.

40) Adapted from *Paper Pilgrimage* by Lawrence Osborne (London, Daybreak, 1990) pp 15–16.

41) Ideas in this section are drawn from Herman Riffel's book; see note 33 above, and from our personal contact with him.

CHAPTER SIX

1) Proverbs 24:3,4. The Hebrew word *byith* means house, household, family. It is important how we build our 'house'. This metaphor is used frequently in Scripture, e.g. Psalm 127:1; Proverbs 9:1; 14:1; 17:1; Matthew 7:24–28; 1 Corinthians 3:10–15.

2) Psychiatrist Eric Berne coined this term. He defined a *game* as: 'A set of transactions between people, which are superficially plausible, but have concealed motivation', i.e. social interactions characterised by ulterior quality and psychological pay-off. See: *Games People Play*, by Eric Berne (UK and USA, Penguin, 1964).

3) Matthew 26:56.

4) Henri Nouwen, 'Creating True Intimacy', *Sojourners* Magazine, June 1984, p 16.

5) Charles Morris, *Psychology, An Introduction* (New Jersey, Prentice Hall, p 439).

6) The many 'defence mechanisms' are listed in psychology text books. Good summaries in: *Introduction to Psychology and Counselling* by Meier, Minerth and Wichern (Grand Rapids, Baker Books, 1982) chapter 18. *Will The Defence Please Rest* by Les Carter (Grand Rapids, Baker, 1986) explores the problem in marriage.

7) Jesus: Matthew 7:3.

8) Proverbs 18:1 (Good News Bible). See also 2 Timothy 3:1–5.

9) J. and A. Sturt, *Created for Love* op cit, chapter 6.

10) 'Tough Love' was popularised by the organisation known by that name which helps parents deal with intolerable behaviour of rebellious children. See *Tough Love* and *Tough Love Solutions* by Phyllis & David York and Ted Wachtel (New York, Bantam Books, 1983, 1984). James Dobson wrote on this issue in marriage: *Love Must Be Tough – New Hope For Families in Crisis* (Waco, Texas, Word, 1983).

11) Briar Whitehead, *Craving for Love* (Tunbridge Wells, Monarch Publications) p 38. Much has been written about co-dependency since the concept first emerged in 1979 in relation to people living with alcoholics. For further reading: *Co-Dependency, An Emerging Issue, US Journal of Drug and Alcohol Dependency* (Hollywood, Health Communications, 1984).

12) See Ephesians 5:33; 1 Peter 3:7. Respect is expected from both husband and wife.

13) Explored thoroughly in *Craving for Love*, op cit.

14) Harry Schaumburg, *False Intimacy* (Colorado Springs, Navpress, 1992) p 16.

CHAPTER SEVEN

1) Roman statesman, philosopher, orator, tragedian.

2) Paul, Ephesians 4:15.

3) For a clear explanation of this process, see Gerald Egan, 'Helping Clients Construct the Future', pp 273–287, *The Skilled Helper* (Pacific Grove, CA, Brooks/Cole Publishing, Fourth Edition, 1990).

4) Kahlil Gibran, *The Prophet* (London, Heinemann, 1972) pp 16,17.

5) Matthew 7:12.

6) Harville Hendricks, *Getting the Love You Want* (Melbourne, Schwartz and Wilson, 1988).

7) See Philippians 2:3; 'Let each esteem other better than themselves' (KJV). We cannot esteem others *better* than ourselves if we do not already have a healthy self-esteem.

8) See Chapter 2, reference 10.

9) For a moving exposition of this kind of loving see *Unconditional Love* by John Powell (Niles, Illinois, Argus, 1978).

10) Luke 6:38. Other references to the principle of giving: Proverbs 11:25; 22:9; Ecclesiastes 11:1,2; Isaiah 58:10,11; Acts 20:35; 2 Corinthians 8:5,7; 9:6–11.

11) Romans 15:7.

12) Graeme Packer, Auckland, New Zealand, 1995.

13) John Powell: *Will The Real Me Please Stand Up* (Valencia, Tabor Publishing, 1985) p 58.

14) Examples of Jesus expressing feelings: Anger: Mark 3:5; John 2:13–17; Joy: John 15:11; Compassion: Mark 6:34, 8:2; Tiredness: John 4:6; Loneliness: Matthew 26:56; 27:46. Discouragement: John 12:27.

15) Matthew 26:38; Mark 14:34.

16) John 11:35.

17) Stanley Schachter: 'The Interaction of Cognitive and Physiological Determinants of Emotional State', *Social Psychology*, Vol I (New York, Academic Press, 1964).

18) Genesis 3:11–13.

19) See Proverbs 14:10; 1 Corinthians 2:11 (TLB).

20) David and Vera Mace, *How To Have A Happy Marriage* (Nashville, Tennessee, Abingdon, 1977) chapter 15.

CHAPTER EIGHT

1) Sir Cliff Richard, Rock musician at the top of his profession for thirty-five years, from his book *Single-Minded* (London, Hodder & Stoughton, 1988) p 79.

2) See 1 Corinthians 7:7. Paul had probably once been married, because he could not have held such a responsible position in the Jewish community as a single person. But these statements confirm that he chose celibacy at this time.

3) Matthew 19:12.

4) 1 Corinthians 7:7, 25–35.

5) 1 Corinthians 7:38.

6) Helena Wilkinson, *Beyond Singleness* (London, Marshall Pickering, 1995). An insightful look at misconceptions and prejudices about singleness, and positive ways of dealing with them.

7) J. Duin, *Sex and the Single Christian* (London, Marshall Pickering, 1990).

8) Letha Scanzoni & Nancy Hardesty, *All We're Meant To Be* (Waco, Word, 1974) p 157.

9) Helena Wilkinson, op cit, p 28.

10) Examples: Prov 18:1; Rom 15:1; 1 Cor 12:25; 13:5; Gal 5:13 (cp v 20); Phil 2:3,4; 2 Tim 3:1–5; James 3:14–16.

11) C.S. Lewis, *A Grief Observed* (London, Faber & Faber, 1961) p 7.

12) See Exodus 22:22,23; Deuteronomy 10:18; Psalm 68:5,6; 146:9; Jeremiah 49:11; James 1:27.

13) Cliff Richard, op cit, chapter 6.

14) Philippians 4:11–13.

15) Adapted from Mike Mason, *The Mystery of Marriage* (Portland, Multnomah, 1985) p 150.

16) Acts 18:1–11.

17) Scott Peck, *Further Along the Road Less Travelled* (New York, Simon and Schuster, 1993) p 13.

18) Peter Lineham, 'The Single Life', in *Sane Sex*, Ed: Francis Foulkes, (Sydney, ANZEA Publishers, 1993) p 69.

19) 1 Corinthians 6:19; 2 Corinthians 6:16.

20) Proverbs 27:17 (GNB).

21) Genesis 2:18.

22) Pierre Teilhard de Chardin, 1881–1955, French philosopher, theologian, palaeontologist.

23) Luke 2:52.
24) Luci Swindoll, *Wide My World Narrow My Bed* (Portland, Multnomah, 1982) p 171.
25) Sheila Pritchard, 'Sexuality and Singleness', in *Sane Sex*, op cit p 86.
26) Philippians 4:11.
27) This suggestion is from *Being Single and Happy*, by Gail Ratcliffe and Hamish Keith (Australia, Simon & Schuster, 1992) p 24.

CHAPTER NINE

1) Ecclesiastes 4:9.
2) Ecclesiastes 4:9 (TLB).
3) Genesis 2:24 (RSV).
4) The concept of 'life scripts' comes from Transactional Analysis Theory.
5) For explanation of this process, see: *Getting the Love You Want* by Harville Hendricks (Melbourne, Schwartz and Wilson, 1988) pp 29–30.
6) Genesis 3:7–10.
7) Edward Shorter, *The Making of the Modern Family* (London, Collins, 1976) p 55.
8) Dan Kiley, *Living Together, Feeling Alone* (New York, Prentice Hall Press, 1989).
9) Explored in *Will The Real Me Please Stand Up* by John Powell and Loretta Brady (Valencia, CA, Tabor, 1985) p 55 ff.
10) Judson Swihart, *How Do You Say I Love You?* (Downers Grove, Ill, Inter Varsity Press, 1979).
11) Gary and Ann-Marie Ezzo, founders of *Growing Kids God's Way*.
12) John Powell, *The Secret of Staying in Love* (Niles, Illinois, Argus Communications, 1974) p 78.
13) Started by Fr Chuck Galagher in New York in the 1960s as a renewal movement for married couples.
14) John Powell, ibid, pp 162–184.
15) Howard and Charlotte Clinebell, *The Intimate Marriage* (Sydney, Family Life Movement of Australia, 1981) chapter 2.
16) Shakespeare: Sonnet 116.
17) David Thomas, *Marital Spirituality* (St Meinrad, Indiana, Abbey Press, 1978) p 78.
18) Tim Hansel, *When I Relax I Feel Guilty* (Elgin, Illinois, David Cook Publishing, 1979). Valuable reading.
19) George Bach, *The Intimate Enemy* (New York, Avon, 1968).

20) Deborah Tannen, *You Just Don't Understand* (Sydney, Random House, 1990). Explores the misunderstandings between men and women in the use of language.

21) David and Vera Mace, *How to Have a Happy Marriage* (Nashville, Abingdon, 1977) chapter 14.

22) Eric Berne, *Games People Play* (New York, Penguin Books, 1964) p 114.

23) For a fuller exegesis: 'The Head of the Epistles' by Berkeley and Alvera Micklesen, *Christianity Today*, Feb 20, 981, pp 20–23.

24) Mark 10:41–45.

25) Howard and Charlotte Clinebell, op cit, p 132.

26) a) *Intended for Pleasure* by Dr Ed and Gay Wheat (New Jersey, Flemming Revell Company, 1977).

b) *The Gift of Sex, A Gift for All Ages, Restoring the Pleasure*, all by Clifford and Joyce Penner (Waco, Word Publishing, 1981, 1986, 1993).

c) *The Act of Marriage* by Tim La Haye (Grand Rapids, Zondervan, 1976).

27) Examples: Genesis 4:1, 25; Matthew 1:25. (The KJV preserves the word 'knew', not used in modern versions.)

28) 1 Corinthians 7:4,5.

29) Clinebell, op cit, p 156.

30) Matthew 18:20.

31) Matthew 18:19.

32) a) *Solomon on Sex* by Joseph Dillow (Nashville, Thomas Nelson, 1977).

b) *A Song for Lovers* by Craig Glickman (Downers Grove, InterVarsity Press, 1976).

c) *Biblical Lovemaking* by Arnold Fruchtenbaum (San Antonia, Ariel Press, 1983).

CHAPTER TEN

1) James 4:8.

2) Henri Nouwen, 'Creating True Intimacy', *Sojourners*, June 1985, p 18.

3) Kenneth Leech, *Soul Friend* (San Francisco, Harper, 1992).

4) St Augustine.

5) Luke 10:27.

6) Isaiah 41:8; James 2:23; Exodus 33:11.

7) John 15:14,15.

8) See Mark 10:17–22.

9) Luke 10:38–42.

10) Psalm 25:14 (RSV, TLB).

11) John 5:39.

12) Song of Solomon 2:16; 5:16; 6:3; 7:10; Jeremiah 31:3; Hosea 2:19.
13) Deuteronomy 7:7,8.
14) Song of Solomon 7:10.
15) John 1:1,14; 14:8,9.
16) See Psalms: Love (118:1); Anger (109:6f); Delight (119:16); Depression (42:5,6); Joy (81:1); Fear (56:3); Desire (84:2); Anguish (38:8); Relaxation (131:2); Loneliness (102:7).
17) Philippians 3:8 (italics ours) and 17.
18) Brother Lawrence, *The Practice of the Presence of God* (London, Mowbrays, 1980).
19) See *When The Well Runs Dry* by Thomas Green (Notre Dame, Ave Maria Press, 1979).
20) See *Interior Castle Explored* by Ruth Burrows (London, Sheed and Ward, 1981).
21) William Barry, *God's Passionate Desire* (Notre Dame, Ave Maria Press, 1993) p 54.
22) Peter discovered his sinfulness: Luke 5:8; the power of Satan over him: Matthew 16:23; his incompetence: Matthew 17:4.
23) Thomas Merton, quoted from Peter Spink in *The Path of the Mystic* (London, Darton, Longman and Todd, 1983) p 125.
24) See: J.B. Phillips, *Your God is Too Small* (London, Epworth, 1952).
25) Romans 8:26.
26) James 4:8. See also Hebrews 10:22.
27) John 3:16; 1 John 4:7–10.
28) Joshua 1:8; Psalms 1:2; 119:15, 27, 78, 99, 148.
29) Psalm 145:5.
30) Richard Foster, *Prayer* (London, Hodder and Stoughton, 1992) p 153.
31) Sister Margaret Magdalen, *Jesus, Man of Prayer* (London, Hodder and Stoughton, 1987) p 99.
32) Contrast Romans 1:25 with Philippians 1:21.
33) Joyce Huggett, *Listening to God* (London, Hodder and Stoughton, 1986).
34) Psalm 46:10.
35) Jim Borst, *Coming to God* (Guildford, Eagle, 1990).
36) Jenny Cooke, from *Keeping a Spiritual Journal*, edited by Edward England (Crowborough, Highland, 1991) p 203.
37) 1 Corinthians 7:32–35.
38) Ephesians 5:32; Revelation 19:7.
39) Isaiah 54:5; Jeremiah 3:14; Hosea 2:16, 19; 2 Corinthians 11:2.
40) Temple Gairdner, 1873–1928, missionary to Egypt, from his diary.

APPENDIX TWO

INTIMACY SURVEY

In order to obtain some objective data on intimacy, we conducted a postal survey of 300 people in New Zealand. Participants were drawn mainly from those who attended various seminars and workshops of ours over a two-year period. Some were students at Bible colleges, and others were personal friends. Forms were returned anonymously. There was about a ten per cent return rate from those who initially agreed to participate in the survey.

Respondents were asked to define intimacy in their own words, as well as aspects of intimacy that were important to them. They were asked questions about their experience of intimacy in their family of origin, their experience of loneliness, friendship, and cross-cultural relationships. Married respondents were asked to define the quality of intimacy they expected in marriage, and the degree to which their experience matched this. Details about specific questions and the results are mentioned throughout the book. Essay questions were analysed by attributing a number to each aspect of the answer, and these were then collated.

We were surprised by the low return rate, but this probably reflects the personal nature of the questions and the degree of commitment needed to think through the answers. This was not a random population sample, because participants were drawn mainly from groups of Christians. However, the survey represents a wide coverage of age, gender, education, denomination, and ethnic background.

The results were computer analysed by Chris Twyman, using Microsoft Access 2.0, which displayed all results as graphs or tables. It is thus possible to compare and contrast all factors. Demographic details are as follows:

Gender   Females 65%; males 35%.

Religion   Although this question was not asked specifically, 89% of respondents indicated by their answers that they had a Christian faith, or at least attended church regularly.

Status   75% were either married or living in a relationship. A few of these were in their second marriage; 7% were divorced or separated; 2% were widowed. 16% of the 300 were single.

Age   The age distribution is shown in Figure 19.

Ethnicity: 72% were New Zealand born 'pakeha', 3% Maori or Pacific Island. Immigrants from: Europe 16%, Australia 5%, Asia 2%, and other 2%.

Statistical analysis: A descriptive analysis method was used to determine the central tendency and variability of the response data, and a 90% confidence interval was used throughout. If further analysis was to be done using other statistical tests, a confidence level of 95% or even 99% would be used.

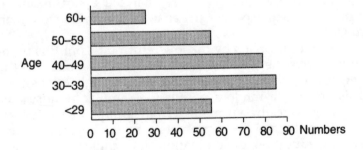

Figure 19. Age distribution of the survey population

A lot of interesting results emerged from this survey, but we only included data relevant to the subject matter of the book. We see this as a sample survey, and that a larger, randomised survey would provide more information and understanding of this topic.

APPENDIX THREE

SELECTED BIBLIOGRAPHY

Friends and Friendship by Jerry and Mary White (Colorado Springs, Navpress, 1982).

A comprehensive study of friendship, containing valuable insights, and defining essential qualities, hindrances and keys to friendship. The implications of friendships to marriage, church life, and between Christians and non-Christians are explored.

Friend of the Lonely Heart by Josh McDowell and Norm Wakefield (Milton Keynes, UK, Word Publishing, 1991).

This racy, readable paperback, aimed at teenagers, provides practical ways of understanding and dealing with the feelings of loneliness that young people face. Concepts are related to the model set by Jesus.

Listening to Others by Joyce Huggett (London, Hodder and Stoughton, 1973).

Writing from deep personal experience, the author describes how she learned to listen to people. Listening with sensitivity to stress, depression and pain in others' lives is a way of loving. She describes the importance of listening to ourselves and to God.

Listening by Anne Long (London, Daybreak, 1990).

A challenging book on the art of listening to myself, others, the world and God. Each section concludes with practical exercises.

People Skills by Robert Bolton, (New Jersey, Prentice-Hall, 1979).

This standard text is a comprehensive coverage of interpersonal communication skills, exploring the essentials of listening, reflecting, assertiveness, and conflict management.

Will The Real Me Please Stand Up by John Powell and Loretta Brady (Valencia, CA, Tabor Publishing, 1985).

Twenty-five Guidelines for Good Communication. The authors describe the principles of how to share oneself and how to accept the sharing of another. A practical book on the skills of good interpersonal communication.

Intimate Partners by Maggie Scarf (New York, Ballantyne Books, 1987).

A powerful book exploring patterns of loving relationships. It is not written from a Christian perspective, but is helpful for couples wanting a more intimate relationship, and for people involved in couple counselling.

Sacrament of Sexuality by Morton and Barbara Kelsey (New York, Amity House, 1986).

A mine of good information, written from a Christian and a psychological perspective. It provides a practical theology of sexuality and love, and valid information on healthy sexuality as well as deviant sex.

Life Path: Personal and Spiritual Growth through Journal Writing by Luci Shaw (Portland, Multnomah, 1991).

This delightful book is a practical guide to using a journal effectively. It is full of insights from the author, and others who have used a journal in their emotional and spiritual growth, with many useful exercises.

The Meaning of Persons by Paul Tournier (London, SCM Press, 1957).

Reflections of a deeply-committed Christian doctor on

the question, 'Who am I?' He clarifies two aspects of personality: the 'Person' (self of reality) and the 'Personage'
(self-picture). Understanding this helps integration of the
personality.

The Christian Vision – The Truth that Sets Us Free by John
Powell (Allen, Texas, Argus Communications, 1984).

A challenging look at understanding yourself, others, the
world, God, suffering, the Church and the will of God. Full
of insights that will stretch you in assessing your values and
making changes.

Getting the Love You Want by Harville Hendricks (Melbourne,
Schwartz and Wilson, 1988).

This bestseller explains how to move from an unconscious
marriage pattern to a conscious marriage, understanding
yourself and how to change destructive behaviour. Some
superb exercises for couples to use to bring this about and
meet each other's needs.

Created for Love by John and Agnes Sturt (Guildford, Eagle,
1994).

This book addresses the issue of self-esteem, from a
psychological and biblical perspective. Practical ways of
growing in self-esteem are described. It is a work-book,
designed for use by individuals on their own, with a counsellor or in a growth/home group.

The Intimate Marriage by Howard and Charlotte Clinebell
(Sydney, Family Life Movement of Australia, 1981).

An excellent coverage of keys and barriers to intimacy.
It focuses on the importance of developing intimacy with
yourself, essential to developing interpersonal intimacy. A
work-book, offering helpful exercises at the end of each
chapter.

Men and Masculinity by Roy McCloughry (London, Hodder
& Stoughton, 1992).

A wide-ranging look at maleness and what it means to

be a man in today's world from a Christian perspective. The sections on men and communication, friendship, sexuality and intimacy are particularly relevant to the thesis of this book.

Exploring Prayer Series, edited by Joyce Huggett (Guildford, Eagle, 1993). These books are particularly relevant to chapter ten.

Patterns Not Padlocks by Angela Ashwin – Prayer for parents and busy people.

Coming to God by James Borst – Using stillness, quiet and contemplation.

The Sounds of God by Michael Mitton – Hearing God's voice.

Spiritual Friendship by Wendy Miller – A guide for prayer companions and friends.

Finding God in the Fast Lane by Joyce Huggett – as well as in life's lay-bys.

Finding the Still Point by Gerald O'Mahony – making use of moods.

Streams in a Dry Land by Heather Ward – Praying when God is distant.

God's Joyful Surprise by Sue Monk Kidd (San Francisco, Harper, 1987).

A delightful, easy to read guide to experiencing God in deepening ways. The author describes her journey from 'doing' to 'being'. Her creative use of everyday experiences encourages the reader to go on this quest for intimacy with God.

APPENDIX FOUR
SCRIPTURE REFERENCES

Old Testament

GENESIS	1:26,27,28,31; 2:7,18,24; 3:7–10,11,13,16; 4:7; 12:10–20; 20:1–18; 26:7–11.
EXODUS	22:22,23; 33:11.
LEVITICUS	19:18.
DEUTERONOMY	7:7,8; 8:2; 10:18; 13:6; 24:1–4.
JOSHUA	1:8.
RUTH	1:16,17.
2 SAMUEL	18:1.
1 KINGS	Ch 18, 19.
PSALM	1:2; 14:1; 15:2; 18:1; 25:14; 38:8; 42:5,6; 46:10; 56:3; 68:5,6; 81:1; 84:2,5–7; 102:7; 109:6f; 111:10; 119:15,16,27,78,99,148; 127:1; 131:2; 139:1,16,23; 145:5; 146:9.
PROVERBS	1:7; 3:5; 9:1,10; 11:25; 13:17; 14:1,10,27; 15:33; 17:1,17; 18:1; 19:4,6,7; 22:9; 24:3,4; 27:17.
ECCLESIASTES	1:14,17; 2:11,17,26; 4:4,6,8–12; 11:1,2.
SONG OF SOLOMON	2:19; 5:16; 6:3; 7:10.
ISAIAH	5:8; 30:15; 33:6; 41:8; 54:5; 58:10,11.
JEREMIAH	1:5; 2:13; 3:14; 31:3; 49:11.
EZEKIEL	36:26.
HOSEA	2:16,19.

New Testament

MATTHEW	5:8; 7:3,12,24–28; 13:12; 18:19,20; 19:3,7,8,10,12; 22:39; 26:13,38,56; 27:46.
MARK	1:35; 3:5; 4:34; 6:34; 8:2; 10:17–22,41–45; 12:31; 14:34,50.
LUKE	1:35; 2:52; 6:12,38; 7:37–50; 10:27,38–42; 23:46; 24:13–22.

JOHN	1:1,18; 2:13–17; 3:16, 34; 4:3–30; 5:39; 6:66; 7:5; 8:1–11, 32–36; 11:35; 12:27; 13:1,23,34; 14:8,9; 15:11,13,14,15; 16:13; 17:3; 19:25–27; 20:2,17; 21:7,20,15–17.
ACTS	18:1–11; 20:35.
ROMANS	1:25; 8:26; 10:9; 12:3,6; 13:9; 15:1,7.
1 CORINTHIANS	2:11; 3:10–15; 6:19; 7:4,5,7,25–35; 9:5; 7:38; 12:12–31; 13:5,7.
2 CORINTHIANS	3:10–15,18; 6:16; 8:5,7; 9:6–11; 11:2; 13:5.
GALATIANS	1:15; 3:28; 5:13,14,20,22,23.
EPHESIANS	1:17,21; 4:13,15; 5:21–33.
PHILIPPIANS	1:21; 2:3,4,21; 3:8,10,17; 4:8,11–13.
2 TIMOTHY	3:1–5.
HEBREWS	4:12,15; 10:22; 13:5;
JAMES	1:4,19,27; 2:8,23; 3:4–16; 4:8.
1 PETER	3:6,7.
2 PETER	2:6.
1 JOHN	4:7–18.
REVELATION	3:20; 19:7.

CREATED FOR LOVE

John and Agnes Sturt

'People with low self-esteem carry around a constant pain inside them which produces self-preoccupation. True self-worth,' assert the authors, 'starts with the awareness of being created in the image of God and being of great value and worth to him.'

Drawing upon the Sturt's many years' counselling experience *Created for Love* is a practical manual for anyone who wants to develop better self-esteem or help others achieve it, offering advice on how to enter into more secure relationships and demonstrating how a lifetime's behavioural patterns can be changed.

'You want the truth? Most of us don't like ourselves very much. And we suspect that God doesn't either . . . Do yourself a favour. Read this book and let the Sturt's insights work magic on your soul.'
John Cooney, Grapevine

'*Created for Love* is a tool that will effect long-lasting and much-needed transformation of body, mind and spirit.'
Joyce Huggett

'Helpful reading . . . I recommend it highly.'
Evangelism today

0 86347 164 1
Eagle